Biblical Counseling Practicum
Making Connections and Working through Cases from a Biblical Framework Perspective

Dr. Nicolas Ellen

Biblical Counseling Practicum:
Making Connections and Working through Cases from a Biblical Framework Perspective

Copyright © 2009 by Dr. Nicolas Ellen

All rights reserved in all countries. No part of this material may be reproduced, stored in a retrieval system, or transmitted in any form or by any means electronic, mechanical, photocopying, recording, or otherwise without prior written permission of the author, publisher and/or copyright owners, except as provided by USA copyright law.

Readers may order copies by visiting www.mycounselingcorner.com

Published and Printed By Expository Counseling Center
Houston, Texas

Unless otherwise noted, scripture references are taken from the New American Standard Bible. © The Lockman Foundation, 1960, 1962, 1963, 1968, 1971, 1972, 1973, 1975, 1977.

Publisher's Cataloging in Publication

Ellen, Nicolas: *Biblical Counseling Practicum*
1. Counseling 2. Christian Counseling 3. Christianity 4. Discipleship

ISBN 978-0-9779692-3-4

Preface

This workbook has been developed to help you learn how to take the basic principles of biblical counseling and put them to practice. The primary focus of this workbook is to help you to learn how to practice Biblical Framework Counseling. If you are not familiar with the teachings of the Biblical Framework, I would encourage you to purchase the book <u>The Heart of Man and The Mental Disorders</u> by Rich Thomson or purchase his 12 set CDs on the topic called Principles of Biblical counseling, or even purchase <u>Biblical Framework Counseling</u> by Nicolas Ellen. Basic information about the Biblical Framework is found in the appendix of this workbook along with some other essential information to help you learn how to work through a counseling case. May this be a tool to truly develop you in the process of doing biblical counselng.

(Go to www.biblicalframeworkcounsleing.org to purchase <u>The Heart of Man and The Mental Disorders</u> Book and CD Set. Go to www.mycounselingcorner.com to purchase Biblical Framework Counseling.)

Make the Connection

When evaluating a situation, you have come to learn what you can and cannot control. The things we cannot control such as people's thoughts, words, actions, or the outcome of situations are what we define as neutral items. They are neutral in that we cannot determine or control these things. They are outside of our power or will. The things we can control such as our own thoughts, words, or actions we define as voluntary actions. Our voluntary actions are either unloving or loving. We have also learned that there are things that happen within our souls beyond our control as a result of our unloving or loving thoughts, words, or actions, such as, a sense of guilt, apparently uncaused fear, apparently uncaused desire to flee leading to fleeing when no one is pursuing, peace of God, confidence before God, and the desire to draw near to God leading to drawing near to God. We have come to define these as involuntary experiences (by-products of our unloving or loving thoughts, words, actions within our soul beyond our control). As you start counseling, you will be challenged to make connections between these things. You will learn to train your mind to analyze the situation, categorize the elements of the situation according to the proper expression on the framework, and place those expressions on the framework accordingly so that you can move towards giving a proper Biblical Solution. In summary, you will learn to make the connections so you can provide the Biblical solutions.

We have provided exercises to help you learn how to make connections so that you can be efficient and effective in doing your cases and practicing biblical counseling in real time. Your assignment is to make the connection between particular items according to the categories and process you have learned from the Biblical Framework. You will put those items in the proper place on the framework and show how they connect to each other according to the framework using arrows. You will gain points according to how well you make the connections. Here are a few examples:

1. Make the connection between disagreement in a marriage, and a spouse committing adultery.
    a. Analyze – What are the two things I am connecting? I am seeking to connect the correlation between someone having a disagreement in their marriage then running off and committing adultery.
    b. Categorize—A disagreement is neutral because it is neither right nor wrong to have a disagreement; committing adultery is a sin but it is a

two-level sin in that it is used to flee from the unloving attitude words, or actions
c. Place on the framework-

Neutral (disagreement) ←——— Lack of Love ——→ Sense of Guilt ——→ Apparently Uncaused Fear ——→ Apparently uncaused fleeing (Adultery)
in response to
the disagreement

2. Make the connection between sinful anger, and experiencing anxiety.
   a. Analyze – What are the two things I am making the connection between? I am seeking to connect the correlation between someone walking in sinful anger and experiencing anxiety.
   b. Categorize- Sinful anger is a lack of love for God and others; anxiety is an expression of apparently uncaused fear
   c. Place on the framework-

Lack of Love (sinful anger) ——→ Sense of Guilt ——→ Apparently Uncaused Fear (Anxiety)

3. Make the connection between a friend saying mean things to a person, and that person being down on himself.
   a. Analyze- What are the two things I am making the connection between? I am seeking to connect the correlation between a friend saying mean things to a person and the person they spoke to being down on self
   b. Categorize – Even though the person saying something mean is unloving, it is an unloving act that is beyond the other person's control; That makes it neutral to the other person because he cannot do anything to stop his friend from saying mean things; However, the fact that he is down on himself because of what his friend is saying is really not about his friend but is an expression of a sense of guilt he has in his heart as a result of having a lack of love towards his friend for what his friend said to him that was mean.
   c. Place on the framework-

Neutral (friend saying mean things) ←——— Lack of Love ——→ Sense of Guilt (Being Down on Self
in response to   as a result of the lack
the friend saying   of love response)
mean things

The arrows to the left indicate that one had to make a voluntary choice in response to the neutral situation (←———). The arrows to the right indicate the involuntary experiences that happened as a result of the voluntary choices (——→). Your goal is to draw out the connection as far as the connection goes between the categories using the arrows to show the connection on the framework. For instance, if the two categories go as far as neutral and apparently uncaused fear, you would draw the arrows to show the connection between the neutral item, and the expression of uncaused fear. For each item and arrow you put in the right place you get 1 point. Let's score the examples we have already done:

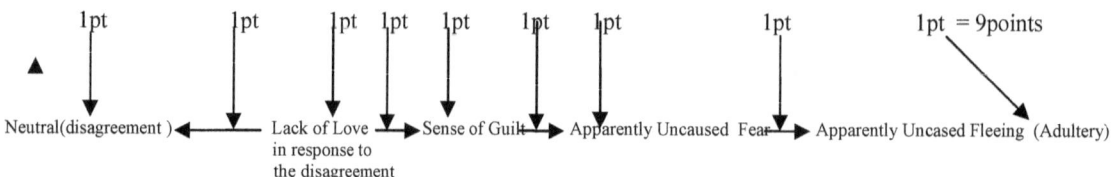

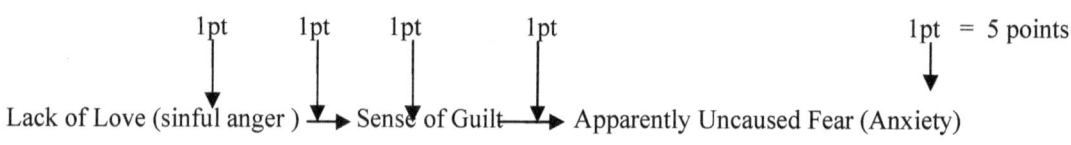

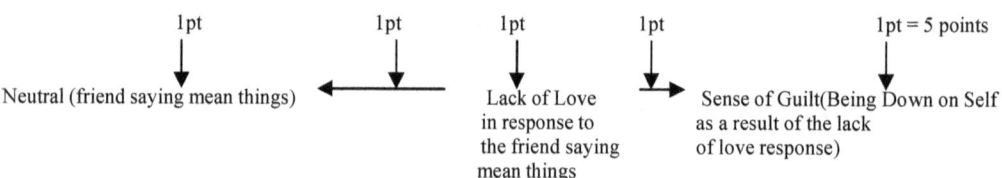

Before you begin to work the make the connection exercises try this one to make sure you understand:

1. Make the connection between missing the bus and having an anxiety attack (worth 7points)

    a. Analyze – What are the two things I am making the connection between?

    b. Categorize-

    c. Place on the framework-

If you did it right you should have something like this:

   a. Analyze – I am making the correlation between a person missing the bus and that person having an anxiety attack

   b. Categorize- missing the bus is neither right nor wrong in and of itself even though it can have some negative consequences, therefore it is neutral; an anxiety attack is an expression of apparently uncaused fear; He had to have a lack of love response to missing the bus which resulted in apparently uncaused fear(anxiety attack) as a result of the lack love response to missing the bus

c. Place on the framework-

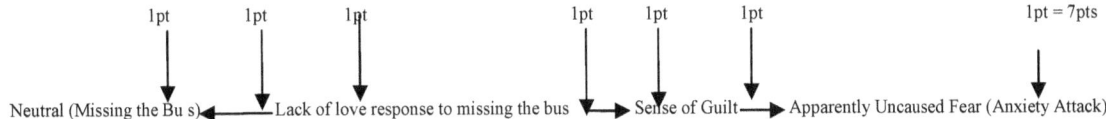

Make the Connection Exercises:

1. Make the connection between missing the bus and having an anxiety attack. (worth 7 points)
    a. Analyze – What are the two things I am making the connection between?

    b. Categorize-

    c. Place on the framework-

2. Make the connection between child being sick and a mother getting drunk. (worth 9 points)
    a. Analyze – What are the two things I am making the connection between?

    b. Categorize-

    c. Place on the framework-

3. Make the connection between worrying and indecisiveness. (worth 5 points)
    a. Analyze – What are the two things I am making the connection between?

    b. Categorize-

    c. Place on the framework-

4. Make the connection between being assigned a task and shunning the responsibility. (worth 9 points)
    a. Analyze – What are the two things I am making the connection between?

    b. Categorize-

    c. Place on the framework-

5. Make the connection between disagreement with spouse and avoiding coming home. (worth 9 points)
    a. Analyze – What are the two things I am making the connection between?

    b. Categorize-

    c. Place on the framework-

6. Make the connection between sinful anger with spouse and committing adultery on spouse. (worth 7 points)
    a. Analyze – What are the two things I am making the connection between?

    b. Categorize-

    c. Place on the framework-

7. Make the connection between boss chastising employee and an employee being panicky. (worth 7 points)
    a. Analyze – What are the two things I am making the connection between?

    b. Categorize-

c. Place on the framework-

8. Make the connection between disappointment of dreams and having suicidal thoughts. (worth 9 points)
    a. Analyze – What are the two things I am making the connection between?

    b. Categorize-

    c. Place on the framework-

9. Make the connection between resentment towards wife and alcoholism. (worth 7 points)
    a. Analyze – What are the two things I am making the connection between?

    b. Categorize-

    c. Place on the framework-

10. Make the connection between unloving parents, and child being rebellious. (worth 9 points)
    a. Analyze – What are the two things I am making the connection between?

    b. Categorize-

    c. Place on the framework-

11. Make the connection between being rejected by others and experiencing restlessness. (worth 7 points)
    a. Analyze – What are the two things I am making the connection between?

    b. Categorize-

    c. Place on the framework-

12. Make the connection between rude boss and an employee constantly being late for work. (worth 9 points)
    a. Analyze – What are the two things I am making the connection between?

    b. Categorize-

    c. Place on the framework-

13. Make the connection between rude to family and feeling down on self. (worth 3 points)
    a. Analyze – What are the two things I am making the connection between?

    b. Categorize-

    c. Place on the framework-

14. Make the connection between disappointment with life and multiple personalities. (worth 9 points)
    a. Analyze – What are the two things I am making the connection between?

    b. Categorize-

    c. Place on the framework-

15. Make the connection between memories of the past, and withdrawing from others. (worth 9 points)
    a. Analyze – What are the two things I am making the connection between?

    b. Categorize-

    c. Place on the framework-

16. Make the connection between bitterness and pursuing homosexual lifestyle. (worth 7 points)
    a. Analyze – What are the two things I am making the connection between?

    b. Categorize-

    c. Place on the framework-

17. Make the connection between jealousy and being angry at self. (worth 3 points)
   a. Analyze – What are the two things I am making the connection between?

   b. Categorize-

   c. Place on the framework-

18. Make the connection between unsinful grief and drug addiction. (worth 9 points)

   a. Analyze – What are the two things I am making the connection between?

   b. Categorize-

   b. Place on the framework-

19. Make the connection between having problems at home and being a workaholic on the job. (worth 9 points)
   a. Analyze – What are the two things I am making the connection between?

   b. Categorize-

   c. Place on the framework-

20. Make the connection between the woman being raped and a woman having suicidal thoughts. (worth 9 points)
    a. Analyze – What are the two things I am making the connection between?

    b. Categorize-

    c. Place on the framework-

21. Make the connection between a friend rejecting a person and the person putting on a façade. (worth 9 points)
    a. Analyze – What are the two things I am making the connection between?

    b. Categorize-

    c. Place on the framework-

22. Make the connection between sibling rejecting his sister and a sister being overly sensitive to criticism. (worth 7 points)
    a. Analyze – What are the two things I am making the connection between?

    b. Categorize-

c. Place on the framework-

23. Make the connection between being abused as a child and becoming schizophrenic. (worth 9 points)
    a. Analyze – What are the two things I am making the connection between?

    b. Categorize-

    c. Place on the framework-

24. Make the connection between being criticized and hesitating to be honest. (worth 7 points)
    a. Analyze – What are the two things I am making the connection between?

    b. Categorize-

    c. Place on the framework-

25. Make the connection between a difficult child life and negative self esteem. (worth 5 points)
    a. Analyze – What are the two things I am making the connection between?

    b. Categorize-

c. Place on the framework-

26. Make the connection between parents fighting and a child having stomach pains. (worth 7 points)
    a. Analyze – What are the two things I am making the connection between?

    b. Categorize-

    c. Place on the framework-

27. Make the connection between mother neglecting child and a child fantasizing about being loved by mother. (worth 9 points)
    a. Analyze – What are the two things I am making the connection between?

    b. Categorize-

    d. Place on the framework-

28. Make the connection between a difficult teacher and a student having excessive perspiration. (worth 7 points)
    a. Analyze – What are the two things I am making the connection between?

b. Categorize-

c. Place on the framework-

29. Make the connection between sinful anger and a depletion of brain chemicals. (worth 5 points)
    a. Analyze – What are the two things I am making the connection between?

    b. Categorize-

    c. Place on the framework-

30. Make the connection between homework not finished and scary nightmares in sleep. (worth 7 points)
    a. Analyze – What are the two things I am making the connection between?

    b. Categorize-

    c. Place on the framework-

31. Make the connection between grumbling and seeking to escape from reality. (worth 7 points)
    a. Analyze – What are the two things I am making the connection between?

    b. Categorize-

c. Place on the framework-

32. Make the connection between discontentment and apprehension. (worth 5 points)
   a. Analyze – What are the two things I am making the connection between?

   b. Categorize-

   c. Place on the framework-

33. Make the connection between bitterness and impotence. (worth 5 points)
   a. Analyze – What are the two things I am making the connection between?

   b. Categorize-

   c. Place on the framework-

34. Make the connection between thoughtlessness and a bothered conscience. (worth 3 points)
   a. Analyze – What are the two things I am making the connection between?

   b. Categorize-

   c. Place on the framework-

35. Make the connection between greed and a sense of worthlessness. (worth 3 points)
    a. Analyze – What are the two things I am making the connection between?

    b. Categorize-

    c. Place on the framework-

36. Make the connection between stubbornness and excessive doubt. (worth 3 points)
    a. Analyze – What are the two things I am making the connection between?

    b. Categorize-

    c. Place on the framework-

37. Make the connection between impatience and defensiveness. (worth 7 points)
    a. Analyze – What are the two things I am making the connection between?

    b. Categorize-

    c. Place on the framework-

38. Make the connection between a tragic situation and living in a fantasy world. (worth 9 points)
    a. Analyze – What are the two things I am making the connection between?

    b. Categorize-

    d. Place on the framework-

39. Make the connection between grudge bearing and impaired concentration. (worth 5 points)
    a. Analyze – What are the two things I am making the connection between?

    b. Categorize-

    c. Place on the framework-

40. Make the connection between envy and refusing to talk to others. (worth 7 points)
    a. Analyze – What are the two things I am making the connection between?

    b. Categorize-

    c. Place on the framework-

41. Make the connection between angry at family and refusing to take a bath. (worth 7 points)
    a. Analyze – What are the two things I am making the connection between?

    b. Categorize-

    c. Place on the framework-

42. Make the connection between worry and over-eating. (worth 7 points)
    a. Analyze – What are the two things I am making the connection between?

    b. Categorize-

    c. Place on the framework-

43. Make the connection between being fired from job and refusing to leave the house. (worth 9 points)
    a. Analyze – What are the two things I am making the connection between?

    b. Categorize-

    c. Place on the framework-

44. Make the connection between disrespectful daughter and a parent having panic attack. (worth 7 points)
    a. Analyze – What are the two things I am making the connection between?

    b. Categorize-

    c. Place on the framework-

45. Make the connection between being discouraged by a friend and feeling down on self. (worth 5 points)
    a. Analyze – What are the two things I am making the connection between?

    b. Categorize-

    c. Place on the framework-

46. Make the connection between losing a job and having seizures. (worth 7 points)
    a. Analyze – What are the two things I am making the connection between?

    b. Categorize-

    c. Place on the framework-

47. Make the connection between making a bad grade and suicide ideation. (worth 9 points)
    a. Analyze – What are the two things I am making the connection between?

    b. Categorize-

    c. Place on the framework-

48. Make the connection between not getting a promotion and an imagination of illness. (worth 7 points)
    a. Analyze – What are the two things I am making the connection between?

    b. Categorize-

    c. Place on the framework-

49. Make the connection between being asked a question and having amnesia. (worth 9 points)
    a. Analyze – What are the two things I am making the connection between?

    b. Categorize-

    c. Place on the framework-

50. Make the connection between unkindness and an unwillingness to reason. (worth 7 points)
   a. Analyze – What are the two things I am making the connection between?

   b. Categorize-

   c. Place on the framework-

Case Studies

Now that you have worked through the making the connection exercises it is time for you to begin working through cases. As you work through these cases try to think in terms of observation, interpretation and application. Observe the case looking for any expression of apparently uncaused fleeing, apparently uncaused fear, and a sense of guilt you can find. Do not try to figure out what the case means during this stage. Just write down what you see in terms of those things. After you have made your observations in accordance to these things begin to work on interpretation. Try to understand what the Lack of Love issues could be that are driving the expressions of apparently uncaused fleeing, apparently uncaused fear, and the sense of guilt in the particular case. Evaluate time frames and relationships within the case to determine what you believe the lack of love issues are. Once you have done your observation and interpretation, then move to application. Explain how the person needs to move from being unloving to loving. Identify expressions of love homework assignments that should be given to overcome the problem. Think about future concepts to teach that will assist in overcoming the problem along with the kinds of homework you will use in order to implement those future concepts. As you learn to do this through these cases, you will find yourself moving towards preparation to do real time counseling. May you take on this challenge and cultivate your skill for biblical counseling through this.

Case Study 1

Jim is a 27 year old male who lives in a middle class neighborhood. Jim works for an oil company making a very good living. He has a wife who he has been married to for 4 years. He married her after he graduated from college. For the last two years there has been a change in Jim's behavior. Jim used to be a very calm and relaxed person. Yet over the last two years Jim has had very extreme mood swings. At work Jim seems to be more talkative than ever. He is basically talking too much to the point where people avoid him when they see him. Where he was normally focused on his job he has become easily distracted by unimportant things such as the sound of the air condition, the tapping of shoes, or even the sound of the Xerox machine. At home he is asking his wife to participate in sexual activities that involve other women. He is constantly spending money on shopping sprees causing them to be short at the end of the month to pay bills. This tends to last for two–three months at a time. Then out of nowhere Jim disassociates from co-workers, wife, and friends. He does not talk, nor does he eat much. He talks about suicide and finds it hard to go to sleep at night. Jim will go months without touching his wife or having sex with her. He will even at times take days off from work during this time and sometimes stay in a hotel and not come home. This has been going on for two years. This started around the time Jim found out his wife could not have children.

1. **Connect the specific characteristics of the problem to the Biblical Framework.**

    a. As you look at the characteristics of the situation/problem are there any expressions of uncaused fleeing being demonstrated? If so, write them down.
    _____
    _____
    _____

    b. As you look at the characteristics of the situation/problem are there any expressions of uncaused fear being demonstrated? If so, write them down.
    _____
    _____
    _____

c. As you look at the characteristics of the situation/problem are there any expressions of a sense of guilt being demonstrated? If so, write them down.

___
___
___

d. As you look at the characteristics of the situation/problem are there any secondary unloving/sinful attitudes, words, actions (unloving /sinful attitudes, words or actions being expressed as a result of the main unloving/sinful attitude, word, or action) being demonstrated? If so, write them down.

___
___
___

2. **Identify the Root of the problem. Identify the specific sin (or what we call the lack of love or unloving attitude, word or action towards God or others) you believe is producing the sense of guilt, apparently uncaused fear or apparently uncaused fleeing.**

   a. Is it an unloving/sinful ***attitude*** producing the sense of guilt, apparently uncaused fear or apparently uncaused fleeing? If so write down what the unloving/sinful attitude is. Write down who or what it is towards.

   ___
   ___

   b. Is it unloving/sinful ***communication*** producing the sense of guilt, apparently uncaused fear or apparently uncaused fleeing? If so write down what the unloving/sinful communication is. Write down who or what is it towards.

   ___
   ___

   c. Is it an unloving/sinful ***behavior or lifestyle*** producing the sense of guilt, apparently uncaused fear or apparently uncaused fleeing? If so, write down what the unloving/sinful behavior or lifestyle is.

   ___
   ___

   d. Is it an unloving/sinful ***way of relating*** producing the sense of guilt, apparently uncaused fear or apparently uncaused fleeing? If so write down what the unloving/sinful way of relating it is. Write down who it is towards?

   ___
   ___

   e. Is it an unloving/ sinful ***desire*** producing the sense of guilt, apparently uncaused fear or apparently uncaused fleeing? If so write down what the unloving/sinful desire is. Write down who or what it is towards.

_____
_____

3. **Explain the process of moving the person from practicing that specific sin (or what we call a lack of love, or unloving attitude, word or action towards God or others) to expressing love for God and others.**

   a. What are the specific unloving/ sinful issues that need to be confessed?
   _____
   _____

   b. What do they need to count on being forgiven of by God when they confess?
   _____
   _____

   c. What areas of their life do they need to walk by the Holy Spirit and not carry out the desires of the flesh?
   _____
   _____

   d. As they do this what can they expect from God in this area?
   _____
   _____

4. **Identify key expressions of love homework assignments you would give to help move the person from practicing the specific sin (or what we call a lack of love, or unloving attitude, word or action towards God or others) to expressing love for God and others . Consider the way you would have them implement these expressions within the context of the problem.**

   a. What expressions of love toward God assignments need to be given in this problem/situation and why?
   _____
   _____
   _____
   _____

   b. What expressions of love towards others assignments need to be given in this problem/situation and why?
   _____
   _____
   _____
   _____

5. **Identify further concepts you need to teach the counselee in order to help them work through their problem and walk in love for God and others.**

    a._____

    b._____

    c._____

    d._____

6. **Think about categories of homework to be used to help implement these concepts.**

    a. *<u>Hope Homework</u>* – projects, activities and reading assignments given to help people gain a true hope in Christ in accordance to the problems they are facing

    b. *<u>Doctrinal Homework</u>* – projects, activities, and reading assignments given to help people gain a solid theological understanding of their problems so that they can deal with them properly

    c. *<u>Awareness Homework</u>* – projects, activities, and reading assignments given to help people become aware of their own sinfulness in the problem so that they can stop deceiving themselves about the problem they are facing and own up to it accordingly

    d. *<u>Embracing God Homework</u>* – projects, activities, and reading assignments given to help people to connect with God according to a particular characteristic of God that relates to their problem or sin

    e. *<u>Action Oriented Homework</u>* – projects and activities that lead people to put off particular sinful thoughts, desires, conversations, behavior, and lifestyle and to put on particular godly thoughts, desires, conversations, behavior, and lifestyle according to the situation or problem in order to walk in love for God and others

    f. *<u>Relational Oriented Homework</u>* – projects and activities that lead people to put off unloving relational patterns and move them to relate in open and loving relational patterns towards others within the situation or problem and abroad

(Concept adapted from *<u>Instruments in a Redeemer's Hand</u>* by Paul Tripp)

Case Study 2

Julia is a 19 year old female. She grew up in a home with a mother and no father. They lived in a lower middle class neighborhood. Her mom worked as a clerk in a grocery store. During her life her mom had various men in and out of the house. Some nice some mean. Julia works at a department store making a little above minimum wage. She stays at home with her mom and helps her pay the bills around the home. Her mom noticed that over the last three months that Julia has been coming home later than usual. When she does come home she notices that Julia has been up all night and does not seem to sleep. She is either on the computer or watching TV. Her mom also noticed that Julia is not eating the way she normally eats. On some days she overeats and on other days she does not eat anything at all. Julia has been complaining of how sad she feels about life and living. She has even mentioned wanting to die. Her friends noticed that Julia seems to be distracted when they talk about things. She always seems to be somewhere else. They noticed that whenever, it is time for the night to end Julia finds a way to stay with them and not go home. Her mom began to ease drop on her conversations and she overheard Julia talking about sexual matters and how she hates sex. As Julia's mom started tracking and monitoring these things she notices that these symptoms started and have been increasing since the Mom's new boyfriend has been spending the night.

1. **Connect the specific characteristics of the problem to the Biblical Framework.**

    a. As you look at the characteristics of the situation/problem are there any expressions of uncaused fleeing being demonstrated? If so, write them down.

    _____
    _____
    _____

    b. As you look at the characteristics of the situation/problem are there any expressions of uncaused fear being demonstrated? If so, write them down.

    _____
    _____
    _____

    c. As you look at the characteristics of the situation/problem are there any expressions of a sense of guilt being demonstrated? If so, write them down.

    _____
    _____
    _____

d. As you look at the characteristics of the situation/problem are there any secondary unloving/sinful attitudes, words, actions (unloving /sinful attitudes, words or actions being expressed as a result of the main unloving/sinful attitude, word, or action) being demonstrated? If so, write them down.

_____
_____
_____

2. **Identify the Root of the problem. Identify the specific sin (or what we call the lack of love or unloving attitude, word or action towards God or others) you believe is producing the sense of guilt, apparently uncaused fear or apparently uncaused fleeing.**

   a. Is it an unloving/sinful ***attitude*** producing the sense of guilt, apparently uncaused fear or apparently uncaused fleeing? If so write down what the unloving/sinful attitude is. Write down who or what it is towards.

   _____
   _____

   b. Is it unloving/sinful ***communication*** producing the sense of guilt, apparently uncaused fear or apparently uncaused fleeing? If so write down what the unloving/sinful communication is. Write down who or what is it towards.

   _____
   _____

   c. Is it an unloving/sinful ***behavior or lifestyle*** producing the sense of guilt, apparently uncaused fear or apparently uncaused fleeing? If so, write down what the unloving/sinful behavior or lifestyle is.

   _____
   _____

   d. Is it an unloving/sinful ***way of relating*** producing the sense of guilt, apparently uncaused fear or apparently uncaused fleeing? If so write down what the unloving/sinful way of relating it is. Write down who it is towards?

   _____
   _____

   e. Is it an unloving/ sinful ***desire*** producing the sense of guilt, apparently uncaused fear or apparently uncaused fleeing? If so write down what the unloving/sinful desire is. Write down who or what it is towards.

   _____
   _____

3. **Explain the process of moving the person from practicing that specific sin (or what we call a lack of love, or unloving attitude, word or action towards God or others) to expressing love for God and others.**

   a. What are the specific unloving/ sinful issues that need to be confessed?
   _____
   _____

   b. What do they need to count on being forgiven of by God when they confess?
   _____
   _____

   c. What areas of their life do they need to walk by the Holy Spirit and not carry out the desires of the flesh?
   _____
   _____

   d. As they do this what can they expect from God in this area?
   _____
   _____

4. **Identify key expressions of love homework assignments you would give to help move the person from practicing the specific sin (or what we call a lack of love, or unloving attitude, word or action towards God or others) to expressing love for God and others. Consider the way you would have them implement these expressions within the context of the problem.**

   a. What expressions of love toward God assignments need to be given in this problem/situation and why?
   _____
   _____
   _____
   _____

   b. What expressions of love towards others assignments need to be given in this problem/situation and why?
   _____
   _____
   _____
   _____

5. **Identify further concepts you need to teach the counselee in order to help them work through their problem and walk in love for God and others.**

    a._____

    b._____

    c._____

    d._____

6. **Think about categories of homework to be used to help implement these concepts.**

    a. *Hope Homework* – projects, activities and reading assignments given to help people gain a true hope in Christ in accordance to the problems they are facing

    b. *Doctrinal Homework* – projects, activities, and reading assignments given to help people gain a solid theological understanding of their problems so that they can deal with them properly

    c. *Awareness Homework* – projects, activities, and reading assignments given to help people become aware of their own sinfulness in the problem so that they can stop deceiving themselves about the problem they are facing and own up to it accordingly

    d. *Embracing God Homework* – projects, activities, and reading assignments given to help people to connect with God according to a particular characteristic of God that relates to their problem or sin

    e. *Action Oriented Homework* – projects and activities that lead people to put off particular sinful thoughts, desires, conversations, behavior, and lifestyle and to put on particular godly thoughts, desires, conversations, behavior, and lifestyle according to the situation or problem in order to walk in love for God and others

    f. *Relational Oriented Homework* – projects and activities that lead people to put off unloving relational patterns and move them to relate in open and loving relational patterns towards others within the situation or problem and abroad

    (Concept adapted from *Instruments in a Redeemer's Hand* by Paul Tripp)

Case Study 3

Kenneth is a 45 year old male. Yesterday he was told by his boss that the company would be downsizing and would no longer be needing his services. Kenneth was not shaken he politely asked when his last day would be and kindly walked out of the office. Over the last few weeks Kenneth has been experiencing many panic attacks on his way to work. His friends report that Kenneth has been eating more than usual, oversleeping and coming in late to work. Kenneth told his friends that the boss has put a camera in Kenneth's house and is watching his every move. Kenneth also believes that his boss has hired hit men to come after him. Kenneth is scared to go outside because he believes his boss is following him. He has been calling in sick and finding reasons why he cannot leave his home. Kenneth has gained about ten pounds in the last five weeks and is refusing to take a bath or clean himself up. Kenneth tries to find every excuse possible not to communicate with his boss.

1. **Connect the specific characteristics of the problem to the Biblical Framework.**

    a. As you look at the characteristics of the situation/problem are there any expressions of uncaused fleeing being demonstrated? If so, write them down.
    _____
    _____
    _____

    b. As you look at the characteristics of the situation/problem are there any expressions of uncaused fear being demonstrated? If so, write them down.
    _____
    _____
    _____

    c. As you look at the characteristics of the situation/problem are there any expressions of a sense of guilt being demonstrated? If so, write them down.
    _____
    _____
    _____

    d. As you look at the characteristics of the situation/problem are there any secondary unloving/sinful attitudes, words, actions (unloving /sinful attitudes, words or actions being expressed as a result of the main unloving/sinful attitude, word, or action) being demonstrated? If so, write them down.
    _____
    _____

2. **Identify the Root of the problem. Identify the specific sin (or what we call the lack of love or unloving attitude, word or action towards God or others) you believe is producing the sense of guilt, apparently uncaused fear or apparently uncaused fleeing.**

   a. Is it an unloving/sinful ***attitude*** producing the sense of guilt, apparently uncaused fear or apparently uncaused fleeing? If so write down what the unloving/sinful attitude is. Write down who or what it is towards.
   _____
   _____

   b. Is it unloving/sinful ***communication*** producing the sense of guilt, apparently uncaused fear or apparently uncaused fleeing? If so write down what the unloving/sinful communication is. Write down who or what is it towards.
   _____
   _____

   c. Is it an unloving/sinful ***behavior or lifestyle*** producing the sense of guilt, apparently uncaused fear or apparently uncaused fleeing? If so, write down what the unloving/sinful behavior or lifestyle is.
   _____
   _____

   d. Is it an unloving/sinful ***way of relating*** producing the sense of guilt, apparently uncaused fear or apparently uncaused fleeing? If so write down what the unloving/sinful way of relating it is. Write down who it is towards?
   _____
   _____

   e. Is it an unloving/ sinful ***desire*** producing the sense of guilt, apparently uncaused fear or apparently uncaused fleeing? If so write down what the unloving/sinful desire is. Write down who or what it is towards.
   _____
   _____

3. **Explain the process of moving the person from practicing that specific sin (or what we call a lack of love, or unloving attitude, word or action towards God or others) to expressing love for God and others.**

   a. What are the specific unloving/ sinful issues that need to be confessed?
   _____
   _____

b. What do they need to count on being forgiven of by God when they confess?

_____
_____

c. What areas of their life do they need to walk by the Holy Spirit and not carry out the desires of the flesh?

_____
_____

d. As they do this what can they expect from God in this area?

_____
_____

4. **Identify key expressions of love homework assignments you would give to help move the person from practicing the specific sin (or what we call a lack of love, or unloving attitude, word or action towards God or others) to expressing love for God and others. Consider the way you would have them implement these expressions within the context of the problem.**

    a. What expressions of love toward God assignments need to be given in this problem/situation and why?

    _____
    _____
    _____
    _____

    b. What expressions of love towards others assignments need to be given in this problem/situation and why?

    _____
    _____
    _____
    _____

5. **Identify further concepts you need to teach the counselee in order to help them work through their problem and walk in love for God and others.**

    a._____

    b._____

    c._____

    d._____

6. **Think about categories of homework to be used to help implement these concepts.**

   a. *Hope Homework* – projects, activities and reading assignments given to help people gain a true hope in Christ in accordance to the problems they are facing

   b. *Doctrinal Homework* – projects, activities, and reading assignments given to help people gain a solid theological understanding of their problems so that they can deal with them properly

   c. *Awareness Homework* – projects, activities, and reading assignments given to help people become aware of their own sinfulness in the problem so that they can stop deceiving themselves about the problem they are facing and own up to it accordingly

   d. *Embracing God Homework* – projects, activities, and reading assignments given to help people to connect with God according to a particular characteristic of God that relates to their problem or sin

   e. *Action Oriented Homework* – projects and activities that lead people to put off particular sinful thoughts, desires, conversations, behavior, and lifestyle and to put on particular godly thoughts, desires, conversations, behavior, and lifestyle according to the situation or problem in order to walk in love for God and others

   f. *Relational Oriented Homework* – projects and activities that lead people to put off unloving relational patterns and move them to relate in open and loving relational patterns towards others within the situation or problem and abroad

(Concept adapted from *Instruments in a Redeemer's Hand* by Paul Tripp)

Case 4

Phil and Erica have been married for 10 years. They met in college where they instantly became good friends. After two years of friendship they decided to get married. Their marriage has had its challenges but the relationship is stable. Over the last few weeks Phil has been avoiding communication with Erica. He simply does not want to talk. He has been coming home later than usual around the time Erica is going to bed or has fallen asleep. Phil has mentioned to his friends that when he is on his way home he experiences panic attacks. So instead of going home he finds himself stopping at the local strip club before he gets home. Lately when he talks to his wife he gets this overwhelming compulsion to clean the house from top to bottom and to take several baths within an hour of their conversation. His wife does not understand what is happening with Phil. She mentioned that this all started around the time Erica acknowledged that she was pregnant.

1. **Connect the specific characteristics of the problem to the Biblical Framework.**

    a. As you look at the characteristics of the situation/problem are there any expressions of uncaused fleeing being demonstrated? If so, write them down.

    _____
    _____
    _____

    b. As you look at the characteristics of the situation/problem are there any expressions of uncaused fear being demonstrated? If so, write them down.

    _____
    _____
    _____

    c. As you look at the characteristics of the situation/problem are there any expressions of a sense of guilt being demonstrated? If so, write them down.

    _____
    _____
    _____

    d. As you look at the characteristics of the situation/problem are there any secondary unloving/sinful attitudes, words, actions (unloving /sinful attitudes, words or actions being expressed as a result of the main unloving/sinful attitude, word, or action) being demonstrated? If so, write them down.

    _____
    _____
    _____

2. **Identify the Root of the problem. Identify the specific sin (or what we call the lack of love or unloving attitude, word or action towards God or others) you believe is producing the sense of guilt, apparently uncaused fear or apparently uncaused fleeing.**

   a. Is it an unloving/sinful ***attitude*** producing the sense of guilt, apparently uncaused fear or apparently uncaused fleeing? If so write down what the unloving/sinful attitude is. Write down who or what it is towards.
   _____
   _____

   b. Is it unloving/sinful ***communication*** producing the sense of guilt, apparently uncaused fear or apparently uncaused fleeing? If so write down what the unloving/sinful communication is. Write down who or what is it towards.
   _____
   _____

   c. Is it an unloving/sinful ***behavior or lifestyle*** producing the sense of guilt, apparently uncaused fear or apparently uncaused fleeing? If so, write down what the unloving/sinful behavior or lifestyle is.
   _____
   _____

   d. Is it an unloving/sinful ***way of relating*** producing the sense of guilt, apparently uncaused fear or apparently uncaused fleeing? If so write down what the unloving/sinful way of relating it is. Write down who it is towards?
   _____
   _____

   e. Is it an unloving/ sinful ***desire*** producing the sense of guilt, apparently uncaused fear or apparently uncaused fleeing? If so write down what the unloving/sinful desire is. Write down who or what it is towards.
   _____
   _____

3. **Explain the process of moving the person from practicing that specific sin (or what we call a lack of love, or unloving attitude, word or action towards God or others) to expressing love for God and others.**

   a. What are the specific unloving/ sinful issues that need to be confessed?
   _____
   _____

b. What do they need to count on being forgiven of by God when they confess?

c. What areas of their life do they need to walk by the Holy Spirit and not carry out the desires of the flesh?

d. As they do this what can they expect from God in this area?

4. **Identify key expressions of love homework assignments you would give to help move the person from practicing the specific sin (or what we call a lack of love, or unloving attitude, word or action towards God or others) to expressing love for God and others. Consider the way you would have them implement these expressions within the context of the problem.**

    a. What expressions of love toward God assignments need to be given in this problem/situation and why?

    b. What expressions of love towards others assignments need to be given in this problem/situation and why?

5. **Identify further concepts you need to teach the counselee in order to help them work through their problem and walk in love for God and others.**

    a.

    b.

    c.

    d.

6. **Think about categories of homework to be used to help implement these concepts.**

    a. *__Hope Homework__* – projects, activities and reading assignments given to help people gain a true hope in Christ in accordance to the problems they are facing

    b. *__Doctrinal Homework__* – projects, activities, and reading assignments given to help people gain a solid theological understanding of their problems so that they can deal with them properly

    c. *__Awareness Homework__* – projects, activities, and reading assignments given to help people become aware of their own sinfulness in the problem so that they can stop deceiving themselves about the problem they are facing and own up to it accordingly

    d. *__Embracing God Homework__* – projects, activities, and reading assignments given to help people to connect with God according to a particular characteristic of God that relates to their problem or sin

    e. *__Action Oriented Homework__* – projects and activities that lead people to put off particular sinful thoughts, desires, conversations, behavior, and lifestyle and to put on particular godly thoughts, desires, conversations, behavior, and lifestyle according to the situation or problem in order to walk in love for God and others

    f. *__Relational Oriented Homework__* – projects and activities that lead people to put off unloving relational patterns and move them to relate in open and loving relational patterns towards others within the situation or problem and abroad

(Concept adapted from *Instruments in a Redeemer's Hand* by Paul Tripp)

Case 5

John is a 15 year old male. John is a freshman in high school. John makes good grades in school and seems to be liked by all. He is respected by his peers and encouraged by his teachers. Lately, John has been having fantasies about killing hitchhikers and cutting open their bodies and eating their insides. In class he seems easily distracted by the sights, sounds and symbols around him such as computers, the sound of the chalk when it hits the board or even the chewing of gum. His friend happened to pass by his locker and noticed that John had a DVD of gay pornography. It made sense to his friend because he noticed that John had been hanging around the guys in the school who were known homosexuals. When confronted by his friend John just simply stated "You don't understand!" John seems to be withdrawing from his close friends and spending more time around the guys who are known homosexuals. His fantasies have even included ways of killing his mother and eating her insides. John has been focusing a lot on suicide and pursuing websites that talk about ways to do so. John smiles a lot on the outside but feels extreme sadness on the inside. John shared with one of his close friends before he caught himself "Sometimes I wish I could just disappear." This all started around the time John's mother put his father out and asked for a divorce from his father.

1. **Connect the specific characteristics of the problem to the Biblical Framework.**

    a. As you look at the characteristics of the situation/problem are there any expressions of uncaused fleeing being demonstrated? If so, write them down.
    _____
    _____
    _____

    b. As you look at the characteristics of the situation/problem are there any expressions of uncaused fear being demonstrated? If so, write them down.
    _____
    _____
    _____

    c. As you look at the characteristics of the situation/problem are there any expressions of a sense of guilt being demonstrated? If so, write them down.
    _____
    _____
    _____

    d. As you look at the characteristics of the situation/problem are there any secondary unloving/sinful attitudes, words, actions (unloving /sinful attitudes, words or actions being expressed as a result of the main unloving/sinful attitude, word, or action) being demonstrated? If so, write them down.

_____
_____
_____

2. **Identify the Root of the problem. Identify the specific sin (or what we call the lack of love or unloving attitude, word or action towards God or others) you believe is producing the sense of guilt, apparently uncaused fear or apparently uncaused fleeing.**

    a. Is it an unloving/sinful *__attitude__* producing the sense of guilt, apparently uncaused fear or apparently uncaused fleeing? If so write down what the unloving/sinful attitude is. Write down who or what it is towards.

    _____
    _____

    b. Is it unloving/sinful *__communication__* producing the sense of guilt, apparently uncaused fear or apparently uncaused fleeing? If so write down what the unloving/sinful communication is. Write down who or what is it towards.

    _____
    _____

    c. Is it an unloving/sinful *__behavior or lifestyle__* producing the sense of guilt, apparently uncaused fear or apparently uncaused fleeing? If so, write down what the unloving/sinful behavior or lifestyle is.

    _____
    _____

    d. Is it an unloving/sinful *__way of relating__* producing the sense of guilt, apparently uncaused fear or apparently uncaused fleeing? If so write down what the unloving/sinful way of relating it is. Write down who it is towards?

    _____
    _____

    e. Is it an unloving/ sinful *__desire__* producing the sense of guilt, apparently uncaused fear or apparently uncaused fleeing? If so write down what the unloving/sinful desire is. Write down who or what it is towards.

    _____
    _____

3. **Explain the process of moving the person from practicing that specific sin (or what we call a lack of love, or unloving attitude, word or action towards God or others) to expressing love for God and others.**

   a. What are the specific unloving/ sinful issues that need to be confessed?
   _____
   _____

   b. What do they need to count on being forgiven of by God when they confess?
   _____
   _____

   c. What areas of their life do they need to walk by the Holy Spirit and not carry out the desires of the flesh?
   _____
   _____

   d. As they do this what can they expect from God in this area?
   _____
   _____

4. **Identify key expressions of love homework assignments you would give to help move the person from practicing the specific sin (or what we call a lack of love, or unloving attitude, word or action towards God or others) to expressing love for God and others. Consider the way you would have them implement these expressions within the context of the problem.**

   a. What expressions of love toward God assignments need to be given in this problem/situation and why?
   _____
   _____
   _____
   _____

   b. What expressions of love towards others assignments need to be given in this problem/situation and why?
   _____
   _____
   _____
   _____

5. **Identify further concepts you need to teach the counselee in order to help them work through their problem and walk in love for God and others.**

   a._____

   b._____

   c._____

   d._____

6. **Think about categories of homework to be used to help implement these concepts.**

   a. ***Hope Homework*** – projects, activities and reading assignments given to help people gain a true hope in Christ in accordance to the problems they are facing

   b. ***Doctrinal Homework*** – projects, activities, and reading assignments given to help people gain a solid theological understanding of their problems so that they can deal with them properly

   c. ***Awareness Homework*** – projects, activities, and reading assignments given to help people become aware of their own sinfulness in the problem so that they can stop deceiving themselves about the problem they are facing and own up to it accordingly

   d. ***Embracing God Homework*** – projects, activities, and reading assignments given to help people to connect with God according to a particular characteristic of God that relates to their problem or sin

   e. ***Action Oriented Homework*** – projects and activities that lead people to put off particular sinful thoughts, desires, conversations, behavior, and lifestyle and to put on particular godly thoughts, desires, conversations, behavior, and lifestyle according to the situation or problem in order to walk in love for God and others

   f. ***Relational Oriented Homework*** – projects and activities that lead people to put off unloving relational patterns and move them to relate in open and loving relational patterns towards others within the situation or problem and abroad

   (Concept adapted from *Instruments in a Redeemer's Hand* by Paul Tripp)

Case 6

Brad is ten years old. His mother and father are both loving and supporting parents. His mother is a housewife and his dad works with a major engineering firm. Over the last few months Brad's parents have been called to speak with his teacher and the principal more than 4 times. The teacher mentioned that Brad does not pay close attention to the instructions given by the teacher. He keeps losing his pencils and worksheets when it is time to do his work. She mentioned that Brad can't seem to sit still in his chair. He tends to wander off to talk to others students when it is time to do his work. Brad tends interrupt the teacher and other students when they are trying to discuss the assignments to work on. The teacher also mentioned that he has not turned in any of his homework assignments over the last three days. Yet when Brad is playing video games or watching TV he does not display any of these behaviors.

1. **Connect the specific characteristics of the problem to the Biblical Framework.**

   a. As you look at the characteristics of the situation/problem are there any expressions of uncaused fleeing being demonstrated? If so, write them down.

   _____
   _____
   _____

   b. As you look at the characteristics of the situation/problem are there any expressions of uncaused fear being demonstrated? If so, write them down.

   _____
   _____
   _____

   c. As you look at the characteristics of the situation/problem are there any expressions of a sense of guilt being demonstrated? If so, write them down.

   _____
   _____
   _____

   d. As you look at the characteristics of the situation/problem are there any secondary unloving/sinful attitudes, words, actions (unloving /sinful attitudes, words or actions being expressed as a result of the main unloving/sinful attitude, word, or action) being demonstrated? If so, write them down.

   _____
   _____
   _____

2. **Identify the Root of the problem. Identify the specific sin (or what we call the lack of love or unloving attitude, word or action towards God or others) you believe is producing the sense of guilt, apparently uncaused fear or apparently uncaused fleeing.**

   a. Is it an unloving/sinful ***attitude*** producing the sense of guilt, apparently uncaused fear or apparently uncaused fleeing? If so write down what the unloving/sinful attitude is. Write down who or what it is towards.

   _____
   _____

   b. Is it unloving/sinful ***communication*** producing the sense of guilt, apparently uncaused fear or apparently uncaused fleeing? If so write down what the unloving/sinful communication is. Write down who or what is it towards.

   _____
   _____

   c. Is it an unloving/sinful ***behavior or lifestyle*** producing the sense of guilt, apparently uncaused fear or apparently uncaused fleeing? If so, write down what the unloving/sinful behavior or lifestyle is.

   _____
   _____

   d. Is it an unloving/sinful ***way of relating*** producing the sense of guilt, apparently uncaused fear or apparently uncaused fleeing? If so write down what the unloving/sinful way of relating it is. Write down who it is towards?

   _____
   _____

   e. Is it an unloving/ sinful ***desire*** producing the sense of guilt, apparently uncaused fear or apparently uncaused fleeing? If so write down what the unloving/sinful desire is. Write down who or what it is towards.

   _____
   _____

3. **Explain the process of moving the person from practicing that specific sin (or what we call a lack of love, or unloving attitude, word or action towards God or others) to expressing love for God and others.**

   a. What are the specific unloving/ sinful issues that need to be confessed?

   _____
   _____

b. What do they need to count on being forgiven of by God when they confess?
_____
_____

c. What areas of their life do they need to walk by the Holy Spirit and not carry out the desires of the flesh?
_____
_____

d. As they do this what can they expect from God in this area?
_____
_____

4. **Identify key expressions of love homework assignments you would give to help move the person from practicing the specific sin (or what we call a lack of love, or unloving attitude, word or action towards God or others) to expressing love for God and others . Consider the way you would have them implement these expressions within the context of the problem.**

   a. What expressions of love toward God assignments need to be given in this problem/situation and why?
   _____
   _____
   _____
   _____
   _____

   b. What expressions of love towards others assignments need to be given in this problem/situation and why?
   _____
   _____
   _____
   _____

5. **Identify further concepts you need to teach the counselee in order to help them work through their problem and walk in love for God and others.**

   a._____

   b._____

   c._____

   d._____

6. **Think about categories of homework to be used to help implement these concepts.**

    a. *Hope Homework* – projects, activities and reading assignments given to help people gain a true hope in Christ in accordance to the problems they are facing

    b. *Doctrinal Homework* – projects, activities, and reading assignments given to help people gain a solid theological understanding of their problems so that they can deal with them properly

    c. *Awareness Homework* – projects, activities, and reading assignments given to help people become aware of their own sinfulness in the problem so that they can stop deceiving themselves about the problem they are facing and own up to it accordingly

    d. *Embracing God Homework* – projects, activities, and reading assignments given to help people to connect with God according to a particular characteristic of God that relates to their problem or sin

    e. *Action Oriented Homework* – projects and activities that lead people to put off particular sinful thoughts, desires, conversations, behavior, and lifestyle and to put on particular godly thoughts, desires, conversations, behavior, and lifestyle according to the situation or problem in order to walk in love for God and others

    f. *Relational Oriented Homework* – projects and activities that lead people to put off unloving relational patterns and move them to relate in open and loving relational patterns towards others within the situation or problem and abroad

(Concept adapted from *Instruments in a Redeemer's Hand* by Paul Tripp)

Case 7

Derrick is 17 years old. He lives with his mom and dad. He is a junior in high school. His parents have been encouraging him to consider choosing a college to attend. Derrick is not sure what he wants to do. Over the past few months Derrick has been picking fights with freshman students. He says it is just a way to introduce freshmen to the school. He and is friends have been stealing from local grocery stores. He says it's no big deal. Lately he has been breaking his curfew and staying out to early in the next morning. His parents are trying to confront him and challenge him but he disrespects them and even walks away from the conversation. He and his friends have even engaged in forcing some of the girls who are wanting to be in the in crowd into sexual activity. Derrick is a very smart individual so he uses his intelligence and charm to talk his way out of bad situations with policemen and teachers. The closer Derrick gets to graduation the worse his behavior becomes. His parents had planned to move to another state after the graduation. Derrick does not want them to do so.

1. **Connect the specific characteristics of the problem to the Biblical Framework.**

   a. As you look at the characteristics of the situation/problem are there any expressions of uncaused fleeing being demonstrated? If so, write them down.

   _____
   _____
   _____

   b. As you look at the characteristics of the situation/problem are there any expressions of uncaused fear being demonstrated? If so, write them down.

   _____
   _____
   _____

   c. As you look at the characteristics of the situation/problem are there any expressions of a sense of guilt being demonstrated? If so, write them down.

   _____
   _____
   _____

   d. As you look at the characteristics of the situation/problem are there any secondary unloving/sinful attitudes, words, actions (unloving /sinful attitudes, words or actions being expressed as a result of the main unloving/sinful attitude, word, or action) being demonstrated? If so, write them down.

   _____
   _____

2. **Identify the Root of the problem. Identify the specific sin (or what we call the lack of love or unloving attitude, word or action towards God or others) you believe is producing the sense of guilt, apparently uncaused fear or apparently uncaused fleeing.**

   a. Is it an unloving/sinful ***attitude*** producing the sense of guilt, apparently uncaused fear or apparently uncaused fleeing? If so write down what the unloving/sinful attitude is. Write down who or what it is towards.

   _____
   _____

   b. Is it unloving/sinful ***communication*** producing the sense of guilt, apparently uncaused fear or apparently uncaused fleeing? If so write down what the unloving/sinful communication is. Write down who or what is it towards.

   _____
   _____

   c. Is it an unloving/sinful ***behavior or lifestyle*** producing the sense of guilt, apparently uncaused fear or apparently uncaused fleeing? If so, write down what the unloving/sinful behavior or lifestyle is.

   _____
   _____

   d. Is it an unloving/sinful ***way of relating*** producing the sense of guilt, apparently uncaused fear or apparently uncaused fleeing? If so write down what the unloving/sinful way of relating it is. Write down who it is towards?

   _____
   _____

   e. Is it an unloving/ sinful ***desire*** producing the sense of guilt, apparently uncaused fear or apparently uncaused fleeing? If so write down what the unloving/sinful desire is. Write down who or what it is towards.

   _____
   _____

3. **Explain the process of moving the person from practicing that specific sin (or what we call a lack of love, or unloving attitude, word or action towards God or others) to expressing love for God and others.**

   a. What are the specific unloving/ sinful issues that need to be confessed?

   _____
   _____

b. What do they need to count on being forgiven of by God when they confess?
_____
_____

c. What areas of their life do they need to walk by the Holy Spirit and not carry out the desires of the flesh?
_____
_____

d. As they do this what can they expect from God in this area?
_____
_____

4. **Identify key expressions of love homework assignments you would give to help move the person from practicing the specific sin (or what we call a lack of love, or unloving attitude, word or action towards God or others) to expressing love for God and others. Consider the way you would have them implement these expressions within the context of the problem.**

    a. What expressions of love toward God assignments need to be given in this problem/situation and why?
    _____
    _____
    _____
    _____
    _____

    b. What expressions of love towards others assignments need to be given in this problem/situation and why?
    _____
    _____
    _____
    _____

5. **Identify further concepts you need to teach the counselee in order to help them work through their problem and walk in love for God and others.**

    a._____

    b._____

    c._____

    d._____

6. **Think about categories of homework to be used to help implement these concepts.**

    a. *Hope Homework* – projects, activities and reading assignments given to help people gain a true hope in Christ in accordance to the problems they are facing

    b. *Doctrinal Homework* – projects, activities, and reading assignments given to help people gain a solid theological understanding of their problems so that they can deal with them properly

    c. *Awareness Homework* – projects, activities, and reading assignments given to help people become aware of their own sinfulness in the problem so that they can stop deceiving themselves about the problem they are facing and own up to it accordingly

    d. *Embracing God Homework* – projects, activities, and reading assignments given to help people to connect with God according to a particular characteristic of God that relates to their problem or sin

    e. *Action Oriented Homework* – projects and activities that lead people to put off particular sinful thoughts, desires, conversations, behavior, and lifestyle and to put on particular godly thoughts, desires, conversations, behavior, and lifestyle according to the situation or problem in order to walk in love for God and others

    f. *Relational Oriented Homework* – projects and activities that lead people to put off unloving relational patterns and move them to relate in open and loving relational patterns towards others within the situation or problem and abroad

(Concept adapted from *Instruments in a Redeemer's Hand* by Paul Tripp)

Case 8

Emmit is 40 years old. He is married to betty who is 39 years old. She has a daughter that is 19 years old from a previous marriage who comes to visit from time to time. She lives with her biological father. Emmit has been having a hard time relating properly to his wife. Over the last couple of days things have been very tense between them. Emmit withdraws and goes to read a book or work on other things. He changes the subject when asked certain questions. He is constantly fighting with her and complains of her lack of respect for him and his decisions. He frequently leaves the house and returns very late. He even has a drink or two before he comes home. Emmit complains that when her 19 year old daughter visits his wife tends to disrespect him and favor her. Whenever the daughter is around there is confusion and disorder. His wife blames him for their daughter not staying with them and he challenges her. This behavior has been happening since the daughter has asked to come and live with them.

1. **Connect the specific characteristics of the problem to the Biblical Framework.**

    a. As you look at the characteristics of the situation/problem are there any expressions of uncaused fleeing being demonstrated? If so, write them down.

    _____
    _____
    _____

    b. As you look at the characteristics of the situation/problem are there any expressions of uncaused fear being demonstrated? If so, write them down.

    _____
    _____
    _____

    c. As you look at the characteristics of the situation/problem are there any expressions of a sense of guilt being demonstrated? If so, write them down.

    _____
    _____
    _____

    d. As you look at the characteristics of the situation/problem are there any secondary unloving/sinful attitudes, words, actions (unloving /sinful attitudes, words or actions being expressed as a result of the main unloving/sinful attitude, word, or action) being demonstrated? If so, write them down.

    _____
    _____
    _____

2. **Identify the Root of the problem. Identify the specific sin (or what we call the lack of love or unloving attitude, word or action towards God or others) you believe is producing the sense of guilt, apparently uncaused fear or apparently uncaused fleeing.**

   a. Is it an unloving/sinful ***attitude*** producing the sense of guilt, apparently uncaused fear or apparently uncaused fleeing? If so write down what the unloving/sinful attitude is. Write down who or what it is towards.
   _____
   _____

   b. Is it unloving/sinful ***communication*** producing the sense of guilt, apparently uncaused fear or apparently uncaused fleeing? If so write down what the unloving/sinful communication is. Write down who or what is it towards.
   _____
   _____

   c. Is it an unloving/sinful ***behavior or lifestyle*** producing the sense of guilt, apparently uncaused fear or apparently uncaused fleeing? If so, write down what the unloving/sinful behavior or lifestyle is.
   _____
   _____

   d. Is it an unloving/sinful ***way of relating*** producing the sense of guilt, apparently uncaused fear or apparently uncaused fleeing? If so write down what the unloving/sinful way of relating it is. Write down who it is towards?
   _____
   _____

   e. Is it an unloving/ sinful ***desire*** producing the sense of guilt, apparently uncaused fear or apparently uncaused fleeing? If so write down what the unloving/sinful desire is. Write down who or what it is towards.
   _____
   _____

3. **Explain the process of moving the person from practicing that specific sin (or what we call a lack of love, or unloving attitude, word or action towards God or others) to expressing love for God and others.**

   a. What are the specific unloving/ sinful issues that need to be confessed?
   _____
   _____

b. What do they need to count on being forgiven of by God when they confess?

_____

_____

c. What areas of their life do they need to walk by the Holy Spirit and not carry out the desires of the flesh?

_____

_____

d. As they do this what can they expect from God in this area?

_____

_____

4. **Identify key expressions of love homework assignments you would give to help move the person from practicing the specific sin (or what we call a lack of love, or unloving attitude, word or action towards God or others) to expressing love for God and others. Consider the way you would have them implement these expressions within the context of the problem.**

   a. What expressions of love toward God assignments need to be given in this problem/situation and why?

   _____

   _____

   _____

   _____

   _____

   b. What expressions of love towards others assignments need to be given in this problem/situation and why?

   _____

   _____

   _____

   _____

5. **Identify further concepts you need to teach the counselee in order to help them work through their problem and walk in love for God and others.**

   a. _____

   b. _____

   c. _____

   d. _____

6. **Think about categories of homework to be used to help implement these concepts.**

    a. *Hope Homework* – projects, activities and reading assignments given to help people gain a true hope in Christ in accordance to the problems they are facing

    b. *Doctrinal Homework* – projects, activities, and reading assignments given to help people gain a solid theological understanding of their problems so that they can deal with them properly

    c. *Awareness Homework* – projects, activities, and reading assignments given to help people become aware of their own sinfulness in the problem so that they can stop deceiving themselves about the problem they are facing and own up to it accordingly

    d. *Embracing God Homework* – projects, activities, and reading assignments given to help people to connect with God according to a particular characteristic of God that relates to their problem or sin

    e. *Action Oriented Homework* – projects and activities that lead people to put off particular sinful thoughts, desires, conversations, behavior, and lifestyle and to put on particular godly thoughts, desires, conversations, behavior, and lifestyle according to the situation or problem in order to walk in love for God and others

    f. *Relational Oriented Homework* – projects and activities that lead people to put off unloving relational patterns and move them to relate in open and loving relational patterns towards others within the situation or problem and abroad

(Concept adapted from *Instruments in a Redeemer's Hand* by Paul Tripp)

Case 9

Jenny is a 27 year old who has currently moved in with her mother to save some money in order to purchase her home. Her mom is a widow and welcomed the company. Jenny left home when she graduated from high school, went to college and has been on her own since graduation from college. Since Jenny has been home her mom has noticed some strange attitudes and behaviors. Jenny tends to check to see if the door is locked maybe 10 to 20 times a day when she comes home from work. She will ask her mother the same question about a subject at least 10 times within 30 minutes. Jenny will wash her hands at least 20 times after eating food or touching things within the home. Jenny is very meticulous in her routine of cleaning the house. She will spend at least 10 hours on the weekend cleaning the house from top to bottom. Jenny tends to be preoccupied with security and safety. She has installed a security camera around the house with surveillance tapes to watch the activities around the house. Her mom discovered by accident that Jenny had an abortion because the child was the product of date rape by her ex-boyfriend.

1. **Connect the specific characteristics of the problem to the Biblical Framework.**

   a. As you look at the characteristics of the situation/problem are there any expressions of uncaused fleeing being demonstrated? If so, write them down.

   _____
   _____
   _____

   b. As you look at the characteristics of the situation/problem are there any expressions of uncaused fear being demonstrated? If so, write them down.

   _____
   _____
   _____

   c. As you look at the characteristics of the situation/problem are there any expressions of a sense of guilt being demonstrated? If so, write them down.

   _____
   _____

   d. As you look at the characteristics of the situation/problem are there any secondary unloving/sinful attitudes, words, actions (unloving /sinful attitudes, words or actions being expressed as a result of the main unloving/sinful attitude, word, or action) being demonstrated? If so, write them down.

   _____
   _____

2. **Identify the Root of the problem. Identify the specific sin (or what we call the lack of love or unloving attitude, word or action towards God or others) you believe is producing the sense of guilt, apparently uncaused fear or apparently uncaused fleeing.**

   a. Is it an unloving/sinful ***attitude*** producing the sense of guilt, apparently uncaused fear or apparently uncaused fleeing? If so write down what the unloving/sinful attitude is. Write down who or what it is towards.
   _____
   _____

   b. Is it unloving/sinful ***communication*** producing the sense of guilt, apparently uncaused fear or apparently uncaused fleeing? If so write down what the unloving/sinful communication is. Write down who or what is it towards.
   _____
   _____

   c. Is it an unloving/sinful ***behavior or lifestyle*** producing the sense of guilt, apparently uncaused fear or apparently uncaused fleeing? If so, write down what the unloving/sinful behavior or lifestyle is.
   _____
   _____

   d. Is it an unloving/sinful ***way of relating*** producing the sense of guilt, apparently uncaused fear or apparently uncaused fleeing? If so write down what the unloving/sinful way of relating it is. Write down who it is towards?
   _____
   _____

   e. Is it an unloving/ sinful ***desire*** producing the sense of guilt, apparently uncaused fear or apparently uncaused fleeing? If so write down what the unloving/sinful desire is. Write down who or what it is towards.
   _____
   _____

3. **Explain the process of moving the person from practicing that specific sin (or what we call a lack of love, or unloving attitude, word or action towards God or others) to expressing love for God and others.**

   a. What are the specific unloving/ sinful issues that need to be confessed?
   _____
   _____

b. What do they need to count on being forgiven of by God when they confess?
_____
_____

c. What areas of their life do they need to walk by the Holy Spirit and not carry out the desires of the flesh?
_____
_____

d. As they do this what can they expect from God in this area?
_____
_____

4. **Identify key expressions of love homework assignments you would give to help move the person from practicing the specific sin (or what we call a lack of love, or unloving attitude, word or action towards God or others) to expressing love for God and others . Consider the way you would have them implement these expressions within the context of the problem.**

   a. What expressions of love toward God assignments need to be given in this problem/situation and why?
   _____
   _____
   _____
   _____
   _____

   b. What expressions of love towards others assignments need to be given in this problem/situation and why?
   _____
   _____
   _____
   _____

5. **Identify further concepts you need to teach the counselee in order to help them work through their problem and walk in love for God and others.**

   a. _____

   b. _____

   c. _____

   d. _____

6. **Think about categories of homework to be used to help implement these concepts.**

   a. ***Hope Homework*** – projects, activities and reading assignments given to help people gain a true hope in Christ in accordance to the problems they are facing

   b. ***Doctrinal Homework*** – projects, activities, and reading assignments given to help people gain a solid theological understanding of their problems so that they can deal with them properly

   c. ***Awareness Homework*** – projects, activities, and reading assignments given to help people become aware of their own sinfulness in the problem so that they can stop deceiving themselves about the problem they are facing and own up to it accordingly

   d. ***Embracing God Homework*** – projects, activities, and reading assignments given to help people to connect with God according to a particular characteristic of God that relates to their problem or sin

   e. ***Action Oriented Homework*** – projects and activities that lead people to put off particular sinful thoughts, desires, conversations, behavior, and lifestyle and to put on particular godly thoughts, desires, conversations, behavior, and lifestyle according to the situation or problem in order to walk in love for God and others

   f. ***Relational Oriented Homework*** – projects and activities that lead people to put off unloving relational patterns and move them to relate in open and loving relational patterns towards others within the situation or problem and abroad

(Concept adapted from *Instruments in a Redeemer's Hand* by Paul Tripp)

Case 10

Barry has been working on his job for the last 15 years. He has a really good record and is even been considered for a major promotion. Over the last month on his way to work Barry experiences restlessness and muscle tension. When his boss asks him job related questions he has difficulty concentrating and finds his mind going blank. His coworkers noticed that he gets real irritable when it is time to go into staff meetings. Barry has a hard time falling asleep at night and is very tired in the morning. When Barry comes home he seems to relax but when it is time for work, he finds himself fantasizing about dying. Over the last month Barry has been having difficulty with a co-worker that his boss asked him to train.

1. **Connect the specific characteristics of the problem to the Biblical Framework.**

    a. As you look at the characteristics of the situation/problem are there any expressions of uncaused fleeing being demonstrated? If so, write them down.

    _____
    _____
    _____

    b. As you look at the characteristics of the situation/problem are there any expressions of uncaused fear being demonstrated? If so, write them down.

    _____
    _____
    _____

    c. As you look at the characteristics of the situation/problem are there any expressions of a sense of guilt being demonstrated? If so, write them down.

    _____
    _____
    _____

    d. As you look at the characteristics of the situation/problem are there any secondary unloving/sinful attitudes, words, actions (unloving /sinful attitudes, words or actions being expressed as a result of the main unloving/sinful attitude, word, or action) being demonstrated? If so, write them down.

    _____
    _____
    _____

2. **Identify the Root of the problem. Identify the specific sin (or what we call the lack of love or unloving attitude, word or action towards God or others) you believe is producing the sense of guilt, apparently uncaused fear or apparently uncaused fleeing.**

   a. Is it an unloving/sinful ***attitude*** producing the sense of guilt, apparently uncaused fear or apparently uncaused fleeing? If so write down what the unloving/sinful attitude is. Write down who or what it is towards.

   _____
   _____

   b. Is it unloving/sinful ***communication*** producing the sense of guilt, apparently uncaused fear or apparently uncaused fleeing? If so write down what the unloving/sinful communication is. Write down who or what is it towards.

   _____
   _____

   c. Is it an unloving/sinful ***behavior or lifestyle*** producing the sense of guilt, apparently uncaused fear or apparently uncaused fleeing? If so, write down what the unloving/sinful behavior or lifestyle is.

   _____
   _____

   d. Is it an unloving/sinful ***way of relating*** producing the sense of guilt, apparently uncaused fear or apparently uncaused fleeing? If so write down what the unloving/sinful way of relating it is. Write down who it is towards?

   _____
   _____

   e. Is it an unloving/ sinful ***desire*** producing the sense of guilt, apparently uncaused fear or apparently uncaused fleeing? If so write down what the unloving/sinful desire is. Write down who or what it is towards.

   _____
   _____

3. **Explain the process of moving the person from practicing that specific sin (or what we call a lack of love, or unloving attitude, word or action towards God or others) to expressing love for God and others.**

   a. What are the specific unloving/ sinful issues that need to be confessed?

   _____
   _____

b. What do they need to count on being forgiven of by God when they confess?

_____
_____

c. What areas of their life do they need to walk by the Holy Spirit and not carry out the desires of the flesh?

_____
_____

d. As they do this what can they expect from God in this area?

_____
_____

4. **Identify key expressions of love homework assignments you would give to help move the person from practicing the specific sin (or what we call a lack of love, or unloving attitude, word or action towards God or others) to expressing love for God and others. Consider the way you would have them implement these expressions within the context of the problem.**

   a. What expressions of love toward God assignments need to be given in this problem/situation and why?

   _____
   _____
   _____
   _____

   b. What expressions of love towards others assignments need to be given in this problem/situation and why?

   _____
   _____
   _____
   _____

5. **Identify further concepts you need to teach the counselee in order to help them work through their problem and walk in love for God and others.**

   a._____

   b._____

   c._____

   d._____

6. **Think about categories of homework to be used to help implement these concepts.**

    a. *Hope Homework* – projects, activities and reading assignments given to help people gain a true hope in Christ in accordance to the problems they are facing

    b. *Doctrinal Homework* – projects, activities, and reading assignments given to help people gain a solid theological understanding of their problems so that they can deal with them properly

    c. *Awareness Homework* – projects, activities, and reading assignments given to help people become aware of their own sinfulness in the problem so that they can stop deceiving themselves about the problem they are facing and own up to it accordingly

    d. *Embracing God Homework* – projects, activities, and reading assignments given to help people to connect with God according to a particular characteristic of God that relates to their problem or sin

    e. *Action Oriented Homework* – projects and activities that lead people to put off particular sinful thoughts, desires, conversations, behavior, and lifestyle and to put on particular godly thoughts, desires, conversations, behavior, and lifestyle according to the situation or problem in order to walk in love for God and others

    f. *Relational Oriented Homework* – projects and activities that lead people to put off unloving relational patterns and move them to relate in open and loving relational patterns towards others within the situation or problem and abroad

(Concept adapted from *Instruments in a Redeemer's Hand* by Paul Tripp)

Case 11

Joan is a new mother. Her baby is 3 months old. Whenever Joan is left alone with the baby she finds herself having chills and hot flashes. She has even been encountering shortness of breath with nausea. She has been complaining of chest pains and discomfort over the last 3 months. There has been a few times where she has been feeling dizzy and almost fainted when left with the baby. She has asked her husband to stay with her and the baby. She admits that sometimes she even has fantasies of killing the baby. The husband has taken all the time away from work he can. Joan is now complaining of a lack of energy to take care of the baby by herself.

1. **Connect the specific characteristics of the problem to the Biblical Framework.**

    a. As you look at the characteristics of the situation/problem are there any expressions of uncaused fleeing being demonstrated? If so, write them down.
    _____
    _____
    _____

    b. As you look at the characteristics of the situation/problem are there any expressions of uncaused fear being demonstrated? If so, write them down.
    _____
    _____
    _____

    c. As you look at the characteristics of the situation/problem are there any expressions of a sense of guilt being demonstrated? If so, write them down.
    _____
    _____
    _____

    d. As you look at the characteristics of the situation/problem are there any secondary unloving/sinful attitudes, words, actions (unloving /sinful attitudes, words or actions being expressed as a result of the main unloving/sinful attitude, word, or action) being demonstrated? If so, write them down.
    _____
    _____
    _____

2. **Identify the Root of the problem. Identify the specific sin (or what we call the lack of love or unloving attitude, word or action towards God or others) you believe is producing the sense of guilt, apparently uncaused fear or apparently uncaused fleeing.**

a. Is it an unloving/sinful ***attitude*** producing the sense of guilt, apparently uncaused fear or apparently uncaused fleeing? If so write down what the unloving/sinful attitude is. Write down who or what it is towards.
___
___

b. Is it unloving/sinful ***communication*** producing the sense of guilt, apparently uncaused fear or apparently uncaused fleeing? If so write down what the unloving/sinful communication is. Write down who or what is it towards.
___
___

c. Is it an unloving/sinful ***behavior or lifestyle*** producing the sense of guilt, apparently uncaused fear or apparently uncaused fleeing? If so, write down what the unloving/sinful behavior or lifestyle is.
___
___

d. Is it an unloving/sinful ***way of relating*** producing the sense of guilt, apparently uncaused fear or apparently uncaused fleeing? If so write down what the unloving/sinful way of relating it is. Write down who it is towards?
___
___

e. Is it an unloving/ sinful ***desire*** producing the sense of guilt, apparently uncaused fear or apparently uncaused fleeing? If so write down what the unloving/sinful desire is. Write down who or what it is towards.
___
___

3. **Explain the process of moving the person from practicing that specific sin (or what we call a lack of love, or unloving attitude, word or action towards God or others) to expressing love for God and others.**

    a. What are the specific unloving/ sinful issues that need to be confessed?
    ___
    ___

    b. What do they need to count on being forgiven of by God when they confess?
    ___
    ___

c. What areas of their life do they need to walk by the Holy Spirit and not carry out the desires of the flesh?

_____
_____

d. As they do this what can they expect from God in this area?

_____
_____

4. **Identify key expressions of love homework assignments you would give to help move the person from practicing the specific sin (or what we call a lack of love, or unloving attitude, word or action towards God or others) to expressing love for God and others. Consider the way you would have them implement these expressions within the context of the problem.**

   a. What expressions of love toward God assignments need to be given in this problem/situation and why?

   _____
   _____
   _____
   _____
   _____

   b. What expressions of love towards others assignments need to be given in this problem/situation and why?

   _____
   _____
   _____
   _____

5. **Identify further concepts you need to teach the counselee in order to help them work through their problem and walk in love for God and others.**

   a. _____

   b. _____

   c. _____

   d. _____

6. **Think about categories of homework to be used to help implement these concepts.**

    a. *Hope Homework* – projects, activities and reading assignments given to help people gain a true hope in Christ in accordance to the problems they are facing

    b. *Doctrinal Homework* – projects, activities, and reading assignments given to help people gain a solid theological understanding of their problems so that they can deal with them properly

    c. *Awareness Homework* – projects, activities, and reading assignments given to help people become aware of their own sinfulness in the problem so that they can stop deceiving themselves about the problem they are facing and own up to it accordingly

    d. *Embracing God Homework* – projects, activities, and reading assignments given to help people to connect with God according to a particular characteristic of God that relates to their problem or sin

    e. *Action Oriented Homework* – projects and activities that lead people to put off particular sinful thoughts, desires, conversations, behavior, and lifestyle and to put on particular godly thoughts, desires, conversations, behavior, and lifestyle according to the situation or problem in order to walk in love for God and others

    f. *Relational Oriented Homework* – projects and activities that lead people to put off unloving relational patterns and move them to relate in open and loving relational patterns towards others within the situation or problem and abroad

(Concept adapted from *Instruments in a Redeemer's Hand* by Paul Tripp)

Case 12

Barbara has been living in an apartment with no social connection with family or friends for about 4 years. She does not talk to her family for more than 10 minutes a week. When she is in a social setting she sits in the corner and watches other people and does not interact with others in the setting. She is the first to come and the first to leave a social gathering. If anyone tries to talk to her that she does not know, she starts to stutter and then shuts down. Barbara does not talk much to people on her job. When people try to connect with her on the job she politely smiles and gives short answers. She then figures out a way to get out of the conversation. When she stays away from her house for more than 24 hours she begins to have panic attacks, heart palpitations and even colds sweats. Barbara has been that way since she was raped over 4 years ago.

1. **Connect the specific characteristics of the problem to the Biblical Framework.**

    a. As you look at the characteristics of the situation/problem are there any expressions of uncaused fleeing being demonstrated? If so, write them down.

    _____
    _____
    _____

    b. As you look at the characteristics of the situation/problem are there any expressions of uncaused fear being demonstrated? If so, write them down.

    _____
    _____
    _____

    c. As you look at the characteristics of the situation/problem are there any expressions of a sense of guilt being demonstrated? If so, write them down.

    _____
    _____
    _____

    d. As you look at the characteristics of the situation/problem are there any secondary unloving/sinful attitudes, words, actions (unloving /sinful attitudes, words or actions being expressed as a result of the main unloving/sinful attitude, word, or action) being demonstrated? If so, write them down.

    _____
    _____
    _____

2. **Identify the Root of the problem. Identify the specific sin (or what we call the lack of love or unloving attitude, word or action towards God or others) you believe is producing the sense of guilt, apparently uncaused fear or apparently uncaused fleeing.**

   a. Is it an unloving/sinful ***attitude*** producing the sense of guilt, apparently uncaused fear or apparently uncaused fleeing? If so write down what the unloving/sinful attitude is. Write down who or what it is towards.

   _____
   _____

   b. Is it unloving/sinful ***communication*** producing the sense of guilt, apparently uncaused fear or apparently uncaused fleeing? If so write down what the unloving/sinful communication is. Write down who or what is it towards.

   _____
   _____

   c. Is it an unloving/sinful ***behavior or lifestyle*** producing the sense of guilt, apparently uncaused fear or apparently uncaused fleeing? If so, write down what the unloving/sinful behavior or lifestyle is.

   _____
   _____

   d. Is it an unloving/sinful ***way of relating*** producing the sense of guilt, apparently uncaused fear or apparently uncaused fleeing? If so write down what the unloving/sinful way of relating it is. Write down who it is towards?

   _____
   _____

   e. Is it an unloving/ sinful ***desire*** producing the sense of guilt, apparently uncaused fear or apparently uncaused fleeing? If so write down what the unloving/sinful desire is. Write down who or what it is towards.

   _____
   _____

3. **Explain the process of moving the person from practicing that specific sin (or what we call a lack of love, or unloving attitude, word or action towards God or others) to expressing love for God and others.**

   a. What are the specific unloving/ sinful issues that need to be confessed?

   _____
   _____

b. What do they need to count on being forgiven of by God when they confess?
_____
_____

c. What areas of their life do they need to walk by the Holy Spirit and not carry out the desires of the flesh?
_____
_____

d. As they do this what can they expect from God in this area?
_____
_____

4. **Identify key expressions of love homework assignments you would give to help move the person from practicing the specific sin (or what we call a lack of love, or unloving attitude, word or action towards God or others) to expressing love for God and others. Consider the way you would have them implement these expressions within the context of the problem.**

   a. What expressions of love toward God assignments need to be given in this problem/situation and why?
   _____
   _____
   _____
   _____
   _____

   b. What expressions of love towards others assignments need to be given in this problem/situation and why?
   _____
   _____
   _____
   _____

5. **Identify further concepts you need to teach the counselee in order to help them work through their problem and walk in love for God and others.**

   a._____

   b._____

   c._____

   d._____

6. **Think about categories of homework to be used to help implement these concepts.**

   a. *Hope Homework* – projects, activities and reading assignments given to help people gain a true hope in Christ in accordance to the problems they are facing

   b. *Doctrinal Homework* – projects, activities, and reading assignments given to help people gain a solid theological understanding of their problems so that they can deal with them properly

   c. *Awareness Homework* – projects, activities, and reading assignments given to help people become aware of their own sinfulness in the problem so that they can stop deceiving themselves about the problem they are facing and own up to it accordingly

   d. *Embracing God Homework* – projects, activities, and reading assignments given to help people to connect with God according to a particular characteristic of God that relates to their problem or sin

   e. *Action Oriented Homework* – projects and activities that lead people to put off particular sinful thoughts, desires, conversations, behavior, and lifestyle and to put on particular godly thoughts, desires, conversations, behavior, and lifestyle according to the situation or problem in order to walk in love for God and others

   f. *Relational Oriented Homework* – projects and activities that lead people to put off unloving relational patterns and move them to relate in open and loving relational patterns towards others within the situation or problem and abroad

(Concept adapted from *Instruments in a Redeemer's Hand* by Paul Tripp)

Case 13

Darnell is a 47 year old prosecutor for the state. He has put away many criminals legally and illegally. His motto is the end always justifies the means. In this last case he accepted evidence from a policeman that was planted on the person in order to help the case. The person was sentenced to twenty years in prison. Since the case Darnell has been preoccupied with doubts about the loyalty of the policeman who planted the evidence. He is constantly checking his phones to see if they have been wire tapped. He created ideas in his mind about what the policeman could be plotting and confronted the policeman accordingly. When talking to others, he reads into conversations things that are not true and responds according to his suspicion instead of the truth. His demeanor has moved from calm to nervous and paranoid. He questions all his staff members about their loyalty and honesty. He can't seem to sleep at night thinking about who might be coming after him. He is taking a lot of medication for anxiety.

1. **Connect the specific characteristics of the problem to the Biblical Framework.**

    a. As you look at the characteristics of the situation/problem are there any expressions of uncaused fleeing being demonstrated? If so, write them down.

    _____
    _____
    _____

    b. As you look at the characteristics of the situation/problem are there any expressions of uncaused fear being demonstrated? If so, write them down.

    _____
    _____
    _____

    c. As you look at the characteristics of the situation/problem are there any expressions of a sense of guilt being demonstrated? If so, write them down.

    _____
    _____
    _____

    d. As you look at the characteristics of the situation/problem are there any secondary unloving/sinful attitudes, words, actions (unloving /sinful attitudes, words or actions being expressed as a result of the main unloving/sinful attitude, word, or action) being demonstrated? If so, write them down.

    _____
    _____
    _____

2. **Identify the Root of the problem. Identify the specific sin (or what we call the lack of love or unloving attitude, word or action towards God or others) you believe is producing the sense of guilt, apparently uncaused fear or apparently uncaused fleeing.**

    a. Is it an unloving/sinful ***attitude*** producing the sense of guilt, apparently uncaused fear or apparently uncaused fleeing? If so write down what the unloving/sinful attitude is. Write down who or what it is towards.

    _____
    _____

    b. Is it unloving/sinful ***communication*** producing the sense of guilt, apparently uncaused fear or apparently uncaused fleeing? If so write down what the unloving/sinful communication is. Write down who or what is it towards.

    _____
    _____

    c. Is it an unloving/sinful ***behavior or lifestyle*** producing the sense of guilt, apparently uncaused fear or apparently uncaused fleeing? If so, write down what the unloving/sinful behavior or lifestyle is.

    _____
    _____

    d. Is it an unloving/sinful ***way of relating*** producing the sense of guilt, apparently uncaused fear or apparently uncaused fleeing? If so write down what the unloving/sinful way of relating it is. Write down who it is towards?

    _____
    _____

    e. Is it an unloving/ sinful ***desire*** producing the sense of guilt, apparently uncaused fear or apparently uncaused fleeing? If so write down what the unloving/sinful desire is. Write down who or what it is towards.

    _____
    _____

3. **Explain the process of moving the person from practicing that specific sin (or what we call a lack of love, or unloving attitude, word or action towards God or others) to expressing love for God and others.**

    a. What are the specific unloving/ sinful issues that need to be confessed?

    _____
    _____

b. What do they need to count on being forgiven of by God when they confess?
___
___

c. What areas of their life do they need to walk by the Holy Spirit and not carry out the desires of the flesh?
___
___

d. As they do this what can they expect from God in this area?
___
___

4. **Identify key expressions of love homework assignments you would give to help move the person from practicing the specific sin (or what we call a lack of love, or unloving attitude, word or action towards God or others) to expressing love for God and others. Consider the way you would have them implement these expressions within the context of the problem.**

   a. What expressions of love toward God assignments need to be given in this problem/situation and why?
   ___
   ___
   ___
   ___

   b. What expressions of love towards others assignments need to be given in this problem/situation and why?
   ___
   ___
   ___
   ___

5. **Identify further concepts you need to teach the counselee in order to help them work through their problem and walk in love for God and others.**

   a.___

   b.___

   c.___

   d.___

6. **Think about categories of homework to be used to help implement these concepts.**

    a. *__Hope Homework__* – projects, activities and reading assignments given to help people gain a true hope in Christ in accordance to the problems they are facing

    b. *__Doctrinal Homework__* – projects, activities, and reading assignments given to help people gain a solid theological understanding of their problems so that they can deal with them properly

    c. *__Awareness Homework__* – projects, activities, and reading assignments given to help people become aware of their own sinfulness in the problem so that they can stop deceiving themselves about the problem they are facing and own up to it accordingly

    d. *__Embracing God Homework__* – projects, activities, and reading assignments given to help people to connect with God according to a particular characteristic of God that relates to their problem or sin

    e. *__Action Oriented Homework__* – projects and activities that lead people to put off particular sinful thoughts, desires, conversations, behavior, and lifestyle and to put on particular godly thoughts, desires, conversations, behavior, and lifestyle according to the situation or problem in order to walk in love for God and others

    f. *__Relational Oriented Homework__* – projects and activities that lead people to put off unloving relational patterns and move them to relate in open and loving relational patterns towards others within the situation or problem and abroad

(Concept adapted from *Instruments in a Redeemer's Hand* by Paul Tripp)

Case 14

Debra is 37 years old. In the past 5 years Debra has been in 8 relationships that have ended poorly. Men say that being with Debra is too intense. Debra tends to think that every disagreement is going to end in a break up. In order to keep them from leaving, she tries to provide them whatever they want. One minute she sees the person she's with as the best thing ever. Within hours she sees them as the scum of the earth. When it seems that she is at the end of a relationship she starts self-mutilating or threatening suicide. When Debra does not get her way in a relationship she throws temper tantrums and finds it hard to control herself. She complains of always having empty feelings in all her relationships. Debra is very consumed with herself. Her identity seems to be tied to whatever she believes the person wants her to be. Debra tends to believe that every ex-boyfriend is out to get her. She goes on eating binges when she believes a relationship is going bad. She has gained over 40 pounds in the last five years.

1. **Connect the specific characteristics of the problem to the Biblical Framework.**

    a. As you look at the characteristics of the situation/problem are there any expressions of uncaused fleeing being demonstrated? If so, write them down.

    _____
    _____
    _____

    b. As you look at the characteristics of the situation/problem are there any expressions of uncaused fear being demonstrated? If so, write them down.

    _____
    _____
    _____

    c. As you look at the characteristics of the situation/problem are there any expressions of a sense of guilt being demonstrated? If so, write them down.

    _____
    _____
    _____

    d. As you look at the characteristics of the situation/problem are there any secondary unloving/sinful attitudes, words, actions (unloving /sinful attitudes, words or actions being expressed as a result of the main unloving/sinful attitude, word, or action) being demonstrated? If so, write them down.

    _____
    _____
    _____

2. **Identify the Root of the problem. Identify the specific sin (or what we call the lack of love or unloving attitude, word or action towards God or others) you believe is producing the sense of guilt, apparently uncaused fear or apparently uncaused fleeing.**

    a. Is it an unloving/sinful ***attitude*** producing the sense of guilt, apparently uncaused fear or apparently uncaused fleeing? If so write down what the unloving/sinful attitude is. Write down who or what it is towards.

    _____
    _____

    b. Is it unloving/sinful ***communication*** producing the sense of guilt, apparently uncaused fear or apparently uncaused fleeing? If so write down what the unloving/sinful communication is. Write down who or what is it towards.

    _____
    _____

    c. Is it an unloving/sinful ***behavior or lifestyle*** producing the sense of guilt, apparently uncaused fear or apparently uncaused fleeing? If so, write down what the unloving/sinful behavior or lifestyle is.

    _____
    _____

    d. Is it an unloving/sinful ***way of relating*** producing the sense of guilt, apparently uncaused fear or apparently uncaused fleeing? If so write down what the unloving/sinful way of relating it is. Write down who it is towards?

    _____
    _____

    e. Is it an unloving/ sinful ***desire*** producing the sense of guilt, apparently uncaused fear or apparently uncaused fleeing? If so write down what the unloving/sinful desire is. Write down who or what it is towards.

    _____
    _____

3. **Explain the process of moving the person from practicing that specific sin (or what we call a lack of love, or unloving attitude, word or action towards God or others) to expressing love for God and others.**

    a. What are the specific unloving/ sinful issues that need to be confessed?

    _____
    _____

b. What do they need to count on being forgiven of by God when they confess?
_____
_____

c. What areas of their life do they need to walk by the Holy Spirit and not carry out the desires of the flesh?
_____
_____

d. As they do this what can they expect from God in this area?
_____
_____

4. **Identify key expressions of love homework assignments you would give to help move the person from practicing the specific sin (or what we call a lack of love, or unloving attitude, word or action towards God or others) to expressing love for God and others . Consider the way you would have them implement these expressions within the context of the problem.**

   a. What expressions of love toward God assignments need to be given in this problem/situation and why?
   _____
   _____
   _____
   _____

   b. What expressions of love towards others assignments need to be given in this problem/situation and why?
   _____
   _____
   _____
   _____

5. **Identify further concepts you need to teach the counselee in order to help them work through their problem and walk in love for God and others.**

   a._____

   b._____

   c._____

   d._____

6. **Think about categories of homework to be used to help implement these concepts.**

    a. *Hope Homework* – projects, activities and reading assignments given to help people gain a true hope in Christ in accordance to the problems they are facing

    b. *Doctrinal Homework* – projects, activities, and reading assignments given to help people gain a solid theological understanding of their problems so that they can deal with them properly

    c. *Awareness Homework* – projects, activities, and reading assignments given to help people become aware of their own sinfulness in the problem so that they can stop deceiving themselves about the problem they are facing and own up to it accordingly

    d. *Embracing God Homework* – projects, activities, and reading assignments given to help people to connect with God according to a particular characteristic of God that relates to their problem or sin

    e. *Action Oriented Homework* – projects and activities that lead people to put off particular sinful thoughts, desires, conversations, behavior, and lifestyle and to put on particular godly thoughts, desires, conversations, behavior, and lifestyle according to the situation or problem in order to walk in love for God and others

    f. *Relational Oriented Homework* – projects and activities that lead people to put off unloving relational patterns and move them to relate in open and loving relational patterns towards others within the situation or problem and abroad

(Concept adapted from *Instruments in a Redeemer's Hand* by Paul Tripp)

Case 15

Rita is a 17 year old female. She lives with her mother and her step father. Rita is not comfortable unless she is made the center of attention by her family and friends. She seems to wear seductive clothing and flirts a lot with the guys in her neighborhood. She uses her body and appearance to get attention. Her friends and family know her as the "drama queen." She tends to overact in disappointing situations. She is easily influenced by anyone who will provide her attention. She tends to think that her relationships with others are closer than what they really are. When she talks she is very shallow and lacks detail. She has been this way since the breakup of her mother and biological father.

1. **Connect the specific characteristics of the problem to the Biblical Framework.**

    a. As you look at the characteristics of the situation/problem are there any expressions of uncaused fleeing being demonstrated? If so, write them down.

    _____
    _____
    _____

    b. As you look at the characteristics of the situation/problem are there any expressions of uncaused fear being demonstrated? If so, write them down.

    _____
    _____
    _____

    c. As you look at the characteristics of the situation/problem are there any expressions of a sense of guilt being demonstrated? If so, write them down.

    _____
    _____
    _____

    d. As you look at the characteristics of the situation/problem are there any secondary unloving/sinful attitudes, words, actions (unloving /sinful attitudes, words or actions being expressed as a result of the main unloving/sinful attitude, word, or action) being demonstrated? If so, write them down.

    _____
    _____
    _____

2. **Identify the Root of the problem. Identify the specific sin (or what we call the lack of love or unloving attitude, word or action towards God or others) you believe is producing the sense of guilt, apparently uncaused fear or apparently uncaused fleeing.**

a. Is it an unloving/sinful ***attitude*** producing the sense of guilt, apparently uncaused fear or apparently uncaused fleeing? If so write down what the unloving/sinful attitude is. Write down who or what it is towards.

___

b. Is it unloving/sinful ***communication*** producing the sense of guilt, apparently uncaused fear or apparently uncaused fleeing? If so write down what the unloving/sinful communication is. Write down who or what is it towards.

___

c. Is it an unloving/sinful ***behavior or lifestyle*** producing the sense of guilt, apparently uncaused fear or apparently uncaused fleeing? If so, write down what the unloving/sinful behavior or lifestyle is.

___

d. Is it an unloving/sinful ***way of relating*** producing the sense of guilt, apparently uncaused fear or apparently uncaused fleeing? If so write down what the unloving/sinful way of relating it is. Write down who it is towards?

___

e. Is it an unloving/ sinful ***desire*** producing the sense of guilt, apparently uncaused fear or apparently uncaused fleeing? If so write down what the unloving/sinful desire is. Write down who or what it is towards.

___

3. **Explain the process of moving the person from practicing that specific sin (or what we call a lack of love, or unloving attitude, word or action towards God or others) to expressing love for God and others.**

   a. What are the specific unloving/ sinful issues that need to be confessed?

   ___

   b. What do they need to count on being forgiven of by God when they confess?

   ___

c. What areas of their life do they need to walk by the Holy Spirit and not carry out the desires of the flesh?

d. As they do this what can they expect from God in this area?

4. **Identify key expressions of love homework assignments you would give to help move the person from practicing the specific sin (or what we call a lack of love, or unloving attitude, word or action towards God or others) to expressing love for God and others. Consider the way you would have them implement these expressions within the context of the problem.**

   a. What expressions of love toward God assignments need to be given in this problem/situation and why?

   b. What expressions of love towards others assignments need to be given in this problem/situation and why?

5. **Identify further concepts you need to teach the counselee in order to help them work through their problem and walk in love for God and others.**

   a.

   b.

   c.

   d.

6. **Think about categories of homework to be used to help implement these concepts.**

    a. *<u>Hope Homework</u>* – projects, activities and reading assignments given to help people gain a true hope in Christ in accordance to the problems they are facing

    b. *<u>Doctrinal Homework</u>* – projects, activities, and reading assignments given to help people gain a solid theological understanding of their problems so that they can deal with them properly

    c. *<u>Awareness Homework</u>* – projects, activities, and reading assignments given to help people become aware of their own sinfulness in the problem so that they can stop deceiving themselves about the problem they are facing and own up to it accordingly

    d. *<u>Embracing God Homework</u>* – projects, activities, and reading assignments given to help people to connect with God according to a particular characteristic of God that relates to their problem or sin

    e. *<u>Action Oriented Homework</u>* – projects and activities that lead people to put off particular sinful thoughts, desires, conversations, behavior, and lifestyle and to put on particular godly thoughts, desires, conversations, behavior, and lifestyle according to the situation or problem in order to walk in love for God and others

    f. *<u>Relational Oriented Homework</u>* – projects and activities that lead people to put off unloving relational patterns and move them to relate in open and loving relational patterns towards others within the situation or problem and abroad

(Concept adapted from *<u>Instruments in a Redeemer's Hand</u>* by Paul Tripp)

Case 16

Ethan is a 27 year old male. He works as a supervisor in a local retail shop. Many of the employees have a difficult time working with Ethan. Ethan believes that his position is the most important position and expects everyone else to recognize him and his position. He daydreams of owning the company and people praising him for being a great owner. He believes that he is so above his employees that he only wants to associate with other mangers. He is constantly looking for his team to praise him or acknowledge his skill and insight. He will work his employees overtime if it makes him look good before upper management. He is insensitive to birthdays, or employees who may be sick. He is always comparing himself to others thinking he has the upper hand. Ethan was not always like this. This started after his wife left him for a woman.

1. **Connect the specific characteristics of the problem to the Biblical Framework.**

    a. As you look at the characteristics of the situation/problem are there any expressions of uncaused fleeing being demonstrated? If so, write them down.
    _____
    _____
    _____

    b. As you look at the characteristics of the situation/problem are there any expressions of uncaused fear being demonstrated? If so, write them down.
    _____
    _____
    _____

    c. As you look at the characteristics of the situation/problem are there any expressions of a sense of guilt being demonstrated? If so, write them down.
    _____
    _____
    _____

    d. As you look at the characteristics of the situation/problem are there any secondary unloving/sinful attitudes, words, actions (unloving /sinful attitudes, words or actions being expressed as a result of the main unloving/sinful attitude, word, or action) being demonstrated? If so, write them down.
    _____
    _____
    _____

2. **Identify the Root of the problem. Identify the specific sin (or what we call the lack of love or unloving attitude, word or action towards God or others) you believe is producing the sense of guilt, apparently uncaused fear or apparently uncaused fleeing.**

    a. Is it an unloving/sinful ***attitude*** producing the sense of guilt, apparently uncaused fear or apparently uncaused fleeing? If so write down what the unloving/sinful attitude is. Write down who or what it is towards.

    _____
    _____

    b. Is it unloving/sinful ***communication*** producing the sense of guilt, apparently uncaused fear or apparently uncaused fleeing? If so write down what the unloving/sinful communication is. Write down who or what is it towards.

    _____
    _____

    c. Is it an unloving/sinful ***behavior or lifestyle*** producing the sense of guilt, apparently uncaused fear or apparently uncaused fleeing? If so, write down what the unloving/sinful behavior or lifestyle is.

    _____
    _____

    d. Is it an unloving/sinful ***way of relating*** producing the sense of guilt, apparently uncaused fear or apparently uncaused fleeing? If so write down what the unloving/sinful way of relating it is. Write down who it is towards?

    _____
    _____

    e. Is it an unloving/ sinful ***desire*** producing the sense of guilt, apparently uncaused fear or apparently uncaused fleeing? If so write down what the unloving/sinful desire is. Write down who or what it is towards.

    _____
    _____

3. **Explain the process of moving the person from practicing that specific sin (or what we call a lack of love, or unloving attitude, word or action towards God or others) to expressing love for God and others.**

    a. What are the specific unloving/ sinful issues that need to be confessed?

    _____
    _____

b. What do they need to count on being forgiven of by God when they confess?
_____
_____

c. What areas of their life do they need to walk by the Holy Spirit and not carry out the desires of the flesh?
_____
_____

d. As they do this what can they expect from God in this area?
_____
_____

4. **Identify key expressions of love homework assignments you would give to help move the person from practicing the specific sin (or what we call a lack of love, or unloving attitude, word or action towards God or others) to expressing love for God and others. Consider the way you would have them implement these expressions within the context of the problem.**

   a. What expressions of love toward God assignments need to be given in this problem/situation and why?
   _____
   _____
   _____
   _____

   b. What expressions of love towards others assignments need to be given in this problem/situation and why?
   _____
   _____
   _____
   _____

5. **Identify further concepts you need to teach the counselee in order to help them work through their problem and walk in love for God and others.**

   a._____

   b._____

   c._____

   d._____

6. **Think about categories of homework to be used to help implement these concepts.**

    a. *<u>Hope Homework</u>* – projects, activities and reading assignments given to help people gain a true hope in Christ in accordance to the problems they are facing

    b. *<u>Doctrinal Homework</u>* – projects, activities, and reading assignments given to help people gain a solid theological understanding of their problems so that they can deal with them properly

    c. *<u>Awareness Homework</u>* – projects, activities, and reading assignments given to help people become aware of their own sinfulness in the problem so that they can stop deceiving themselves about the problem they are facing and own up to it accordingly

    d. *<u>Embracing God Homework</u>* – projects, activities, and reading assignments given to help people to connect with God according to a particular characteristic of God that relates to their problem or sin

    e. *<u>Action Oriented Homework</u>* – projects and activities that lead people to put off particular sinful thoughts, desires, conversations, behavior, and lifestyle and to put on particular godly thoughts, desires, conversations, behavior, and lifestyle according to the situation or problem in order to walk in love for God and others

    f. *<u>Relational Oriented Homework</u>* – projects and activities that lead people to put off unloving relational patterns and move them to relate in open and loving relational patterns towards others within the situation or problem and abroad

(Concept adapted from *Instruments in a Redeemer's Hand* by Paul Tripp)

Case 17

Scott has been the pastor of a moderately large church for the past two years. The congregation seems to really enjoy his style of shepherding. Yet, lately Pastor Scott has been acting out of the character people have come to know and love. When it comes to planning activities, Pastor Scott normally focuses on the big picture. Lately he has been so obsessed with every little detail in the activities that people lose focus on what the activity is about. Normally he is able to present sermons and finish them in a timely manner. Lately he has not been able to finish sermons because he has been giving so much detail that his sermons are going past the allotted time and people are having a hard time understanding the point. Pastor Scott normally would delegate work to others so that he can spend time studying. Lately he has been trying to do everything himself without a hint of help from others. He is becoming more rigid and stubborn in what he directs others to do. This all started after his assistant pastor left the church and took over 100 members with him.

1. **Connect the specific characteristics of the problem to the Biblical Framework.**

    a. As you look at the characteristics of the situation/problem are there any expressions of uncaused fleeing being demonstrated? If so, write them down.

    _____
    _____
    _____

    b. As you look at the characteristics of the situation/problem are there any expressions of uncaused fear being demonstrated? If so, write them down.

    _____
    _____
    _____

    c. As you look at the characteristics of the situation/problem are there any expressions of a sense of guilt being demonstrated? If so, write them down.

    _____
    _____
    _____

    d. As you look at the characteristics of the situation/problem are there any secondary unloving/sinful attitudes, words, actions (unloving /sinful attitudes, words or actions being expressed as a result of the main unloving/sinful attitude, word, or action) being demonstrated? If so, write them down.

    _____
    _____
    _____

2. **Identify the Root of the problem. Identify the specific sin (or what we call the lack of love or unloving attitude, word or action towards God or others) you believe is producing the sense of guilt, apparently uncaused fear or apparently uncaused fleeing.**

    a. Is it an unloving/sinful ***attitude*** producing the sense of guilt, apparently uncaused fear or apparently uncaused fleeing? If so write down what the unloving/sinful attitude is. Write down who or what it is towards.

    _____
    _____

    b. Is it unloving/sinful ***communication*** producing the sense of guilt, apparently uncaused fear or apparently uncaused fleeing? If so write down what the unloving/sinful communication is. Write down who or what is it towards.

    _____
    _____

    c. Is it an unloving/sinful ***behavior or lifestyle*** producing the sense of guilt, apparently uncaused fear or apparently uncaused fleeing? If so, write down what the unloving/sinful behavior or lifestyle is.

    _____
    _____

    d. Is it an unloving/sinful ***way of relating*** producing the sense of guilt, apparently uncaused fear or apparently uncaused fleeing? If so write down what the unloving/sinful way of relating it is. Write down who it is towards?

    _____
    _____

    e. Is it an unloving/ sinful ***desire*** producing the sense of guilt, apparently uncaused fear or apparently uncaused fleeing? If so write down what the unloving/sinful desire is. Write down who or what it is towards.

    _____
    _____

3. **Explain the process of moving the person from practicing that specific sin (or what we call a lack of love, or unloving attitude, word or action towards God or others) to expressing love for God and others.**

    a. What are the specific unloving/ sinful issues that need to be confessed?

    _____
    _____

b. What do they need to count on being forgiven of by God when they confess?
_____
_____

c. What areas of their life do they need to walk by the Holy Spirit and not carry out the desires of the flesh?
_____
_____

d. As they do this what can they expect from God in this area?
_____
_____

4. **Identify key expressions of love homework assignments you would give to help move the person from practicing the specific sin (or what we call a lack of love, or unloving attitude, word or action towards God or others) to expressing love for God and others. Consider the way you would have them implement these expressions within the context of the problem.**

   a. What expressions of love toward God assignments need to be given in this problem/situation and why?
   _____
   _____
   _____
   _____
   _____

   b. What expressions of love towards others assignments need to be given in this problem/situation and why?
   _____
   _____
   _____
   _____

5. **Identify further concepts you need to teach the counselee in order to help them work through their problem and walk in love for God and others.**

   a._____

   b._____

   c._____

   d._____

6. **Think about categories of homework to be used to help implement these concepts.**

   a. *Hope Homework* – projects, activities and reading assignments given to help people gain a true hope in Christ in accordance to the problems they are facing

   b. *Doctrinal Homework* – projects, activities, and reading assignments given to help people gain a solid theological understanding of their problems so that they can deal with them properly

   c. *Awareness Homework* – projects, activities, and reading assignments given to help people become aware of their own sinfulness in the problem so that they can stop deceiving themselves about the problem they are facing and own up to it accordingly

   d. *Embracing God Homework* – projects, activities, and reading assignments given to help people to connect with God according to a particular characteristic of God that relates to their problem or sin

   e. *Action Oriented Homework* – projects and activities that lead people to put off particular sinful thoughts, desires, conversations, behavior, and lifestyle and to put on particular godly thoughts, desires, conversations, behavior, and lifestyle according to the situation or problem in order to walk in love for God and others

   f. *Relational Oriented Homework* – projects and activities that lead people to put off unloving relational patterns and move them to relate in open and loving relational patterns towards others within the situation or problem and abroad

(Concept adapted from *Instruments in a Redeemer's Hand* by Paul Tripp)

Case 18

Carl is a great man of God. He has been a faithful servant to his church in so many ways. Everyone knows Carl to be a warm kind and encouraging person. Over the last few weeks Carl has not been himself. Carl has been turning away from ministry work and not attending fellowship with other members. He says that he is just not interested in fellowship or serving. Carl has been lying in bed staying awake at night while sleeping all day. Carl has been losing weight because he refuses to eat. Carl is constantly thinking about ending his life. This all started when Carl discovered that his best friend was having an affair with his wife.

1. **Connect the specific characteristics of the problem to the Biblical Framework.**

   a. As you look at the characteristics of the situation/problem are there any expressions of uncaused fleeing being demonstrated? If so, write them down.

   _____
   _____
   _____

   b. As you look at the characteristics of the situation/problem are there any expressions of uncaused fear being demonstrated? If so, write them down.

   _____
   _____
   _____

   c. As you look at the characteristics of the situation/problem are there any expressions of a sense of guilt being demonstrated? If so, write them down.

   _____
   _____
   _____

   d. As you look at the characteristics of the situation/problem are there any secondary unloving/sinful attitudes, words, actions (unloving /sinful attitudes, words or actions being expressed as a result of the main unloving/sinful attitude, word, or action) being demonstrated? If so, write them down.

   _____
   _____
   _____

2. **Identify the Root of the problem. Identify the specific sin (or what we call the lack of love or unloving attitude, word or action towards God or others) you believe is producing the sense of guilt, apparently uncaused fear or apparently uncaused fleeing.**

a. Is it an unloving/sinful ***attitude*** producing the sense of guilt, apparently uncaused fear or apparently uncaused fleeing? If so write down what the unloving/sinful attitude is. Write down who or what it is towards.

_____
_____

b. Is it unloving/sinful ***communication*** producing the sense of guilt, apparently uncaused fear or apparently uncaused fleeing? If so write down what the unloving/sinful communication is. Write down who or what is it towards.

_____
_____

c. Is it an unloving/sinful ***behavior or lifestyle*** producing the sense of guilt, apparently uncaused fear or apparently uncaused fleeing? If so, write down what the unloving/sinful behavior or lifestyle is.

_____
_____

d. Is it an unloving/sinful ***way of relating*** producing the sense of guilt, apparently uncaused fear or apparently uncaused fleeing? If so write down what the unloving/sinful way of relating it is. Write down who it is towards?

_____
_____

e. Is it an unloving/ sinful ***desire*** producing the sense of guilt, apparently uncaused fear or apparently uncaused fleeing? If so write down what the unloving/sinful desire is. Write down who or what it is towards.

_____
_____

3. **Explain the process of moving the person from practicing that specific sin (or what we call a lack of love, or unloving attitude, word or action towards God or others) to expressing love for God and others.**

    a. What are the specific unloving/ sinful issues that need to be confessed?

    _____
    _____

    b. What do they need to count on being forgiven of by God when they confess?

    _____
    _____

c. What areas of their life do they need to walk by the Holy Spirit and not carry out the desires of the flesh?

_____
_____

d. As they do this what can they expect from God in this area?

_____
_____

4. **Identify key expressions of love homework assignments you would give to help move the person from practicing the specific sin (or what we call a lack of love, or unloving attitude, word or action towards God or others) to expressing love for God and others. Consider the way you would have them implement these expressions within the context of the problem.**

   a. What expressions of love toward God assignments need to be given in this problem/situation and why?

   _____
   _____
   _____
   _____
   _____

   b. What expressions of love towards others assignments need to be given in this problem/situation and why?

   _____
   _____
   _____
   _____

5. **Identify further concepts you need to teach the counselee in order to help them work through their problem and walk in love for God and others.**

   a. _____

   b. _____

   c. _____

   d. _____

6. **Think about categories of homework to be used to help implement these concepts.**

    a. *Hope Homework* – projects, activities and reading assignments given to help people gain a true hope in Christ in accordance to the problems they are facing

    b. *Doctrinal Homework* – projects, activities, and reading assignments given to help people gain a solid theological understanding of their problems so that they can deal with them properly

    c. *Awareness Homework* – projects, activities, and reading assignments given to help people become aware of their own sinfulness in the problem so that they can stop deceiving themselves about the problem they are facing and own up to it accordingly

    d. *Embracing God Homework* – projects, activities, and reading assignments given to help people to connect with God according to a particular characteristic of God that relates to their problem or sin

    e. *Action Oriented Homework* – projects and activities that lead people to put off particular sinful thoughts, desires, conversations, behavior, and lifestyle and to put on particular godly thoughts, desires, conversations, behavior, and lifestyle according to the situation or problem in order to walk in love for God and others

    f. *Relational Oriented Homework* – projects and activities that lead people to put off unloving relational patterns and move them to relate in open and loving relational patterns towards others within the situation or problem and abroad

(Concept adapted from *Instruments in a Redeemer's Hand* by Paul Tripp)

Case 19

Timothy is a 16 year old junior in high school. His school is known for being the trendiest school in the city. If you do not have the latest fashions you are ridiculed and rejected. Timothy avoids connecting with any group in school because he does not want to be criticized. The only people Timothy will hang around are his teachers because they encourage him in his education. He makes sure that when he is around his peers that he does and says the things he knows they would consider cool. Timothy is overly worried about how people view him. As a result, he tries to get to school at the time the bell rings so that he does not have to interact or be seen by others. Timothy over thinks the simplest of conversations and actions. He will rehearse for hours how to say hello in his mirror. He will rehearse for hours how to do certain cool handshakes. Timothy tends to see himself as inferior to other kids his age. If anyone tries to invite Timothy to do something other than what he is used to doing, he will turn it down for fear he may do something stupid and be ridiculed by others. Timothy's Dad used to be in the crowd when he was Timothy's age. Since Timothy has been in high school his dad had been criticizing him for not getting involved with the in crowd. Timothy is constantly experiencing rejection from his dad for not fitting in.

1. **Connect the specific characteristics of the problem to the Biblical Framework.**

    a. As you look at the characteristics of the situation/problem are there any expressions of uncaused fleeing being demonstrated? If so, write them down.

    _____
    _____
    _____

    b. As you look at the characteristics of the situation/problem are there any expressions of uncaused fear being demonstrated? If so, write them down.

    _____
    _____
    _____

    c. As you look at the characteristics of the situation/problem are there any expressions of a sense of guilt being demonstrated? If so, write them down.

    _____
    _____
    _____

d. As you look at the characteristics of the situation/problem are there any secondary unloving/sinful attitudes, words, actions (unloving /sinful attitudes, words or actions being expressed as a result of the main unloving/sinful attitude, word, or action) being demonstrated? If so, write them down.

_____
_____
_____

2. **Identify the Root of the problem. Identify the specific sin (or what we call the lack of love or unloving attitude, word or action towards God or others) you believe is producing the sense of guilt, apparently uncaused fear or apparently uncaused fleeing.**

   a. Is it an unloving/sinful ***attitude*** producing the sense of guilt, apparently uncaused fear or apparently uncaused fleeing? If so write down what the unloving/sinful attitude is. Write down who or what it is towards.

   _____
   _____

   b. Is it unloving/sinful ***communication*** producing the sense of guilt, apparently uncaused fear or apparently uncaused fleeing? If so write down what the unloving/sinful communication is. Write down who or what is it towards.

   _____
   _____

   c. Is it an unloving/sinful ***behavior or lifestyle*** producing the sense of guilt, apparently uncaused fear or apparently uncaused fleeing? If so, write down what the unloving/sinful behavior or lifestyle is.

   _____
   _____

   d. Is it an unloving/sinful ***way of relating*** producing the sense of guilt, apparently uncaused fear or apparently uncaused fleeing? If so write down what the unloving/sinful way of relating it is. Write down who it is towards?

   _____
   _____

   c. Is it an unloving/ sinful ***desire*** producing the sense of guilt, apparently uncaused fear or apparently uncaused fleeing? If so write down what the unloving/sinful desire is. Write down who or what it is towards.

   _____
   _____

3. **Explain the process of moving the person from practicing that specific sin (or what we call a lack of love, or unloving attitude, word or action towards God or others) to expressing love for God and others.**

   a. What are the specific unloving/ sinful issues that need to be confessed?
   _____
   _____

   b. What do they need to count on being forgiven of by God when they confess?
   _____
   _____

   c. What areas of their life do they need to walk by the Holy Spirit and not carry out the desires of the flesh?
   _____
   _____

   d. As they do this what can they expect from God in this area?
   _____
   _____

4. **Identify key expressions of love homework assignments you would give to help move the person from practicing the specific sin (or what we call a lack of love, or unloving attitude, word or action towards God or others) to expressing love for God and others. Consider the way you would have them implement these expressions within the context of the problem.**

   a. What expressions of love toward God assignments need to be given in this problem/situation and why?
   _____
   _____
   _____
   _____

   b. What expressions of love towards others assignments need to be given in this problem/situation and why?
   _____
   _____
   _____

5. **Identify further concepts you need to teach the counselee in order to help them work through their problem and walk in love for God and others.**

   a._____

   b._____

   c._____

   d._____

6. **Think about categories of homework to be used to help implement these concepts.**

   a. ***Hope Homework*** – projects, activities and reading assignments given to help people gain a true hope in Christ in accordance to the problems they are facing

   b. ***Doctrinal Homework*** – projects, activities, and reading assignments given to help people gain a solid theological understanding of their problems so that they can deal with them properly

   c. ***Awareness Homework*** – projects, activities, and reading assignments given to help people become aware of their own sinfulness in the problem so that they can stop deceiving themselves about the problem they are facing and own up to it accordingly

   d. ***Embracing God Homework*** – projects, activities, and reading assignments given to help people to connect with God according to a particular characteristic of God that relates to their problem or sin

   e. ***Action Oriented Homework*** – projects and activities that lead people to put off particular sinful thoughts, desires, conversations, behavior, and lifestyle and to put on particular godly thoughts, desires, conversations, behavior, and lifestyle according to the situation or problem in order to walk in love for God and others

   f. ***Relational Oriented Homework*** – projects and activities that lead people to put off unloving relational patterns and move them to relate in open and loving relational patterns towards others within the situation or problem and abroad

   (Concept adapted from *Instruments in a Redeemer's Hand* by Paul Tripp)

Case 20

Joan is a 24 year old single female. She calls her mom and dad everyday to help her to make all kinds of frivolous decisions about everything from which store she should buy groceries to what kinds of clothes should she be wearing to work. Anytime she does not follow through on an assignment at work she blames it on poor training of the boss or lack of training from parents. She says yes to almost anything and everyone because she does not want to lose their company. Unless you tell Joan to do something she will not initiate any activity or assignment. Generally she tries to find a man who has a high paying job so that he can take care of her. She can't stay in her apartment for more than two days by herself without trying to go stay with her parents or inviting people to come stay at her home. Joan has been this way since she was sixteen. At sixteen Joan was separated for 5 days from her parents on a camping trip. She wandered off into the forest to explore and ended up getting lost. They eventually found her curled up in the fetal position in the middle of the forest.

1. **Connect the specific characteristics of the problem to the Biblical Framework.**

    a. As you look at the characteristics of the situation/problem are there any expressions of uncaused fleeing being demonstrated? If so, write them down.

    _____
    _____
    _____

    b. As you look at the characteristics of the situation/problem are there any expressions of uncaused fear being demonstrated? If so, write them down.

    _____
    _____
    _____

    c. As you look at the characteristics of the situation/problem are there any expressions of a sense of guilt being demonstrated? If so, write them down.

    _____
    _____
    _____

    d. As you look at the characteristics of the situation/problem are there any secondary unloving/sinful attitudes, words, actions (unloving /sinful attitudes, words or actions being expressed as a result of the main unloving/sinful attitude, word, or action) being demonstrated? If so, write them down.

    _____
    _____

2. **Identify the Root of the problem. Identify the specific sin (or what we call the lack of love or unloving attitude, word or action towards God or others) you believe is producing the sense of guilt, apparently uncaused fear or apparently uncaused fleeing.**

   a. Is it an unloving/sinful ***attitude*** producing the sense of guilt, apparently uncaused fear or apparently uncaused fleeing? If so write down what the unloving/sinful attitude is. Write down who or what it is towards.
   _____
   _____

   b. Is it unloving/sinful ***communication*** producing the sense of guilt, apparently uncaused fear or apparently uncaused fleeing? If so write down what the unloving/sinful communication is. Write down who or what is it towards.
   _____
   _____

   c. Is it an unloving/sinful ***behavior or lifestyle*** producing the sense of guilt, apparently uncaused fear or apparently uncaused fleeing? If so, write down what the unloving/sinful behavior or lifestyle is.
   _____
   _____

   d. Is it an unloving/sinful ***way of relating*** producing the sense of guilt, apparently uncaused fear or apparently uncaused fleeing? If so write down what the unloving/sinful way of relating it is. Write down who it is towards?
   _____
   _____

   e. Is it an unloving/ sinful ***desire*** producing the sense of guilt, apparently uncaused fear or apparently uncaused fleeing? If so write down what the unloving/sinful desire is. Write down who or what it is towards.
   _____
   _____

3. **Explain the process of moving the person from practicing that specific sin (or what we call a lack of love, or unloving attitude, word or action towards God or others) to expressing love for God and others.**

   a. What are the specific unloving/ sinful issues that need to be confessed?
   _____
   _____

b. What do they need to count on being forgiven of by God when they confess?
_____
_____

c. What areas of their life do they need to walk by the Holy Spirit and not carry out the desires of the flesh?
_____
_____

d. As they do this what can they expect from God in this area?
_____
_____

4. **Identify key expressions of love homework assignments you would give to help move the person from practicing the specific sin (or what we call a lack of love, or unloving attitude, word or action towards God or others) to expressing love for God and others. Consider the way you would have them implement these expressions within the context of the problem.**

   a. What expressions of love toward God assignments need to be given in this problem/situation and why?
   _____
   _____
   _____
   _____
   _____

   b. What expressions of love towards others assignments need to be given in this problem/situation and why?
   _____
   _____
   _____
   _____

5. **Identify further concepts you need to teach the counselee in order to help them work through their problem and walk in love for God and others.**

   a. _____

   b. _____

   c. _____

   d. _____

6. **Think about categories of homework to be used to help implement these concepts.**

    a. *Hope Homework* – projects, activities and reading assignments given to help people gain a true hope in Christ in accordance to the problems they are facing

    b. *Doctrinal Homework* – projects, activities, and reading assignments given to help people gain a solid theological understanding of their problems so that they can deal with them properly

    c. *Awareness Homework* – projects, activities, and reading assignments given to help people become aware of their own sinfulness in the problem so that they can stop deceiving themselves about the problem they are facing and own up to it accordingly

    d. *Embracing God Homework* – projects, activities, and reading assignments given to help people to connect with God according to a particular characteristic of God that relates to their problem or sin

    e. *Action Oriented Homework* – projects and activities that lead people to put off particular sinful thoughts, desires, conversations, behavior, and lifestyle and to put on particular godly thoughts, desires, conversations, behavior, and lifestyle according to the situation or problem in order to walk in love for God and others

    f. *Relational Oriented Homework* – projects and activities that lead people to put off unloving relational patterns and move them to relate in open and loving relational patterns towards others within the situation or problem and abroad

(Concept adapted from *Instruments in a Redeemer's Hand* by Paul Tripp)

Case 21

David and Carol have been married for 15 years. They have a good marriage. As they have been planning their 15th anniversary David has been acting in ways that are unusual for his character. He has been staying up all night and only getting about 4 hours of sleep. He complains of having racing thoughts that seem to come in and out of his mind. He talks non-stop with his wife for hours without letting her get a word in. So much so that she is worn out from listening. David has been spending money on frivolous items causing Carol to have a shortage in paying bills. Carol noticed that since David has come back from the doctor's office he has had this strange behavior.

1. **Connect the specific characteristics of the problem to the Biblical Framework.**

   a. As you look at the characteristics of the situation/problem are there any expressions of uncaused fleeing being demonstrated? If so, write them down.

   _____
   _____
   _____

   b. As you look at the characteristics of the situation/problem are there any expressions of uncaused fear being demonstrated? If so, write them down.

   _____
   _____
   _____

   c. As you look at the characteristics of the situation/problem are there any expressions of a sense of guilt being demonstrated? If so, write them down.

   _____
   _____
   _____

   d. As you look at the characteristics of the situation/problem are there any secondary unloving/sinful attitudes, words, actions (unloving /sinful attitudes, words or actions being expressed as a result of the main unloving/sinful attitude, word, or action) being demonstrated? If so, write them down.

   _____
   _____
   _____

2. **Identify the Root of the problem. Identify the specific sin (or what we call the lack of love or unloving attitude, word or action towards God or others)**

you believe is producing the sense of guilt, apparently uncaused fear or apparently uncaused fleeing.

   a. Is it an unloving/sinful ***attitude*** producing the sense of guilt, apparently uncaused fear or apparently uncaused fleeing? If so write down what the unloving/sinful attitude is. Write down who or what it is towards.
   _____
   _____

   b. Is it unloving/sinful ***communication*** producing the sense of guilt, apparently uncaused fear or apparently uncaused fleeing? If so write down what the unloving/sinful communication is. Write down who or what is it towards.
   _____
   _____

   c. Is it an unloving/sinful ***behavior or lifestyle*** producing the sense of guilt, apparently uncaused fear or apparently uncaused fleeing? If so, write down what the unloving/sinful behavior or lifestyle is.
   _____
   _____

   d. Is it an unloving/sinful ***way of relating*** producing the sense of guilt, apparently uncaused fear or apparently uncaused fleeing? If so write down what the unloving/sinful way of relating it is. Write down who it is towards?
   _____
   _____

   e. Is it an unloving/ sinful ***desire*** producing the sense of guilt, apparently uncaused fear or apparently uncaused fleeing? If so write down what the unloving/sinful desire is. Write down who or what it is towards.
   _____
   _____

3. **Explain the process of moving the person from practicing that specific sin (or what we call a lack of love, or unloving attitude, word or action towards God or others) to expressing love for God and others.**

   a. What are the specific unloving/ sinful issues that need to be confessed?
   _____
   _____

   b. What do they need to count on being forgiven of by God when they confess?
   _____
   _____

c. What areas of their life do they need to walk by the Holy Spirit and not carry out the desires of the flesh?

_____
_____

d. As they do this what can they expect from God in this area?

_____
_____

4. **Identify key expressions of love homework assignments you would give to help move the person from practicing the specific sin (or what we call a lack of love, or unloving attitude, word or action towards God or others) to expressing love for God and others. Consider the way you would have them implement these expressions within the context of the problem.**

   a. What expressions of love toward God assignments need to be given in this problem/situation and why?

   _____
   _____
   _____
   _____

   b. What expressions of love towards others assignments need to be given in this problem/situation and why?

   _____
   _____
   _____
   _____

5. **Identify further concepts you need to teach the counselee in order to help them work through their problem and walk in love for God and others.**

   a._____

   b._____

   c._____

   d._____

6. **Think about categories of homework to be used to help implement these concepts.**

    a. *<u>Hope Homework</u>* – projects, activities and reading assignments given to help people gain a true hope in Christ in accordance to the problems they are facing

    b. *<u>Doctrinal Homework</u>* – projects, activities, and reading assignments given to help people gain a solid theological understanding of their problems so that they can deal with them properly

    c. *<u>Awareness Homework</u>* – projects, activities, and reading assignments given to help people become aware of their own sinfulness in the problem so that they can stop deceiving themselves about the problem they are facing and own up to it accordingly

    d. *<u>Embracing God Homework</u>* – projects, activities, and reading assignments given to help people to connect with God according to a particular characteristic of God that relates to their problem or sin

    e. *<u>Action Oriented Homework</u>* – projects and activities that lead people to put off particular sinful thoughts, desires, conversations, behavior, and lifestyle and to put on particular godly thoughts, desires, conversations, behavior, and lifestyle according to the situation or problem in order to walk in love for God and others

    f. *<u>Relational Oriented Homework</u>* – projects and activities that lead people to put off unloving relational patterns and move them to relate in open and loving relational patterns towards others within the situation or problem and abroad

(Concept adapted from *Instruments in a Redeemer's Hand* by Paul Tripp)

Case 22

Patrick has fallen into a state of grief. Patrick has not bathed or washed up in days. He has loss interest in playing football with his friends or just hanging out. He is not eating nor is he sleeping. He complains of having empty feelings and even wishing he would die. Patrick finds it hard to concentrate when communicating with others. His friends say that since his grandfather has died Patrick has been acting this way.

1. **Connect the specific characteristics of the problem to the Biblical Framework.**

   a. As you look at the characteristics of the situation/problem are there any expressions of uncaused fleeing being demonstrated? If so, write them down.

   _____
   _____
   _____

   b. As you look at the characteristics of the situation/problem are there any expressions of uncaused fear being demonstrated? If so, write them down.

   _____
   _____
   _____

   c. As you look at the characteristics of the situation/problem are there any expressions of a sense of guilt being demonstrated? If so, write them down.

   _____
   _____
   _____

   d. As you look at the characteristics of the situation/problem are there any secondary unloving/sinful attitudes, words, actions (unloving /sinful attitudes, words or actions being expressed as a result of the main unloving/sinful attitude, word, or action) being demonstrated? If so, write them down.

   _____
   _____
   _____

2. **Identify the Root of the problem. Identify the specific sin (or what we call the lack of love or unloving attitude, word or action towards God or others) you believe is producing the sense of guilt, apparently uncaused fear or apparently uncaused fleeing.**

a. Is it an unloving/sinful ***attitude*** producing the sense of guilt, apparently uncaused fear or apparently uncaused fleeing? If so write down what the unloving/sinful attitude is. Write down who or what it is towards.

_____
_____

b. Is it unloving/sinful ***communication*** producing the sense of guilt, apparently uncaused fear or apparently uncaused fleeing? If so write down what the unloving/sinful communication is. Write down who or what is it towards.

_____
_____

c. Is it an unloving/sinful ***behavior or lifestyle*** producing the sense of guilt, apparently uncaused fear or apparently uncaused fleeing? If so, write down what the unloving/sinful behavior or lifestyle is.

_____
_____

d. Is it an unloving/sinful ***way of relating*** producing the sense of guilt, apparently uncaused fear or apparently uncaused fleeing? If so write down what the unloving/sinful way of relating it is. Write down who it is towards?

_____
_____

e. Is it an unloving/ sinful ***desire*** producing the sense of guilt, apparently uncaused fear or apparently uncaused fleeing? If so write down what the unloving/sinful desire is. Write down who or what it is towards.

_____
_____

3. **Explain the process of moving the person from practicing that specific sin (or what we call a lack of love, or unloving attitude, word or action towards God or others) to expressing love for God and others.**

   a. What are the specific unloving/ sinful issues that need to be confessed?

   _____
   _____

   b. What do they need to count on being forgiven of by God when they confess?

   _____
   _____

c. What areas of their life do they need to walk by the Holy Spirit and not carry out the desires of the flesh?

_____
_____

d. As they do this what can they expect from God in this area?

_____
_____

4. **Identify key expressions of love homework assignments you would give to help move the person from practicing the specific sin (or what we call a lack of love, or unloving attitude, word or action towards God or others) to expressing love for God and others. Consider the way you would have them implement these expressions within the context of the problem.**

   a. What expressions of love toward God assignments need to be given in this problem/situation and why?

   _____
   _____
   _____
   _____
   _____

   b. What expressions of love towards others assignments need to be given in this problem/situation and why?

   _____
   _____
   _____
   _____

5. **Identify further concepts you need to teach the counselee in order to help them work through their problem and walk in love for God and others.**

   a._____

   b._____

   c._____

   d._____

6. **Think about categories of homework to be used to help implement these concepts.**

    a. *Hope Homework* – projects, activities and reading assignments given to help people gain a true hope in Christ in accordance to the problems they are facing

    b. *Doctrinal Homework* – projects, activities, and reading assignments given to help people gain a solid theological understanding of their problems so that they can deal with them properly

    c. *Awareness Homework* – projects, activities, and reading assignments given to help people become aware of their own sinfulness in the problem so that they can stop deceiving themselves about the problem they are facing and own up to it accordingly

    d. *Embracing God Homework* – projects, activities, and reading assignments given to help people to connect with God according to a particular characteristic of God that relates to their problem or sin

    e. *Action Oriented Homework* – projects and activities that lead people to put off particular sinful thoughts, desires, conversations, behavior, and lifestyle and to put on particular godly thoughts, desires, conversations, behavior, and lifestyle according to the situation or problem in order to walk in love for God and others

    f. *Relational Oriented Homework* – projects and activities that lead people to put off unloving relational patterns and move them to relate in open and loving relational patterns towards others within the situation or problem and abroad

(Concept adapted from *Instruments in a Redeemer's Hand* by Paul Tripp)

Case 23

Susan is a 35 years old single female. She works as a paralegal for a major law firm. Lately Susan has been having recurrent thoughts of death and dying. She also finds herself having anxiety attacks at random times during the week. Susan seems to be preoccupied with someone or something coming to get her. Susan has been washing her hands to the point of scarring. She checks her door at night at least 40 times during the night. Susan checks her car doors at least 20 times a day to make sure that they are locked while she is at work. All this has been taking place since Susan's boss has hired a new paralegal and asked her to work alongside Susan.

1. **Connect the specific characteristics of the problem to the Biblical Framework.**

   a. As you look at the characteristics of the situation/problem are there any expressions of uncaused fleeing being demonstrated? If so, write them down.
   _____
   _____
   _____

   b. As you look at the characteristics of the situation/problem are there any expressions of uncaused fear being demonstrated? If so, write them down.
   _____
   _____
   _____

   c. As you look at the characteristics of the situation/problem are there any expressions of a sense of guilt being demonstrated? If so, write them down.
   _____
   _____
   _____

   d. As you look at the characteristics of the situation/problem are there any secondary unloving/sinful attitudes, words, actions (unloving /sinful attitudes, words or actions being expressed as a result of the main unloving/sinful attitude, word, or action) being demonstrated? If so, write them down.
   _____
   _____
   _____

2. **Identify the Root of the problem. Identify the specific sin (or what we call the lack of love or unloving attitude, word or action towards God or others)**

you believe is producing the sense of guilt, apparently uncaused fear or apparently uncaused fleeing.

   a. Is it an unloving/sinful ***attitude*** producing the sense of guilt, apparently uncaused fear or apparently uncaused fleeing? If so write down what the unloving/sinful attitude is. Write down who or what it is towards.
   _____
   _____

   b. Is it unloving/sinful ***communication*** producing the sense of guilt, apparently uncaused fear or apparently uncaused fleeing? If so write down what the unloving/sinful communication is. Write down who or what is it towards.
   _____
   _____

   c. Is it an unloving/sinful ***behavior or lifestyle*** producing the sense of guilt, apparently uncaused fear or apparently uncaused fleeing? If so, write down what the unloving/sinful behavior or lifestyle is.
   _____
   _____

   d. Is it an unloving/sinful ***way of relating*** producing the sense of guilt, apparently uncaused fear or apparently uncaused fleeing? If so write down what the unloving/sinful way of relating it is. Write down who it is towards?
   _____
   _____

   e. Is it an unloving/ sinful ***desire*** producing the sense of guilt, apparently uncaused fear or apparently uncaused fleeing? If so write down what the unloving/sinful desire is. Write down who or what it is towards.
   _____
   _____

3. **Explain the process of moving the person from practicing that specific sin (or what we call a lack of love, or unloving attitude, word or action towards God or others) to expressing love for God and others.**

   a. What are the specific unloving/ sinful issues that need to be confessed?
   _____
   _____

   b. What do they need to count on being forgiven of by God when they confess?
   _____
   _____

c. What areas of their life do they need to walk by the Holy Spirit and not carry out the desires of the flesh?

_____
_____

d. As they do this what can they expect from God in this area?

_____
_____

4. **Identify key expressions of love homework assignments you would give to help move the person from practicing the specific sin (or what we call a lack of love, or unloving attitude, word or action towards God or others) to expressing love for God and others. Consider the way you would have them implement these expressions within the context of the problem.**

   a. What expressions of love toward God assignments need to be given in this problem/situation and why?

   _____
   _____
   _____
   _____
   _____

   b. What expressions of love towards others assignments need to be given in this problem/situation and why?

   _____
   _____
   _____
   _____

5. **Identify further concepts you need to teach the counselee in order to help them work through their problem and walk in love for God and others.**

   a._____

   b._____

   c._____

   d._____

6. **Think about categories of homework to be used to help implement these concepts.**

   a. *Hope Homework* – projects, activities and reading assignments given to help people gain a true hope in Christ in accordance to the problems they are facing

   b. *Doctrinal Homework* – projects, activities, and reading assignments given to help people gain a solid theological understanding of their problems so that they can deal with them properly

   c. *Awareness Homework* – projects, activities, and reading assignments given to help people become aware of their own sinfulness in the problem so that they can stop deceiving themselves about the problem they are facing and own up to it accordingly

   d. *Embracing God Homework* – projects, activities, and reading assignments given to help people to connect with God according to a particular characteristic of God that relates to their problem or sin

   e. *Action Oriented Homework* – projects and activities that lead people to put off particular sinful thoughts, desires, conversations, behavior, and lifestyle and to put on particular godly thoughts, desires, conversations, behavior, and lifestyle according to the situation or problem in order to walk in love for God and others

   f. *Relational Oriented Homework* – projects and activities that lead people to put off unloving relational patterns and move them to relate in open and loving relational patterns towards others within the situation or problem and abroad

(Concept adapted from *Instruments in a Redeemer's Hand* by Paul Tripp)

Case 24

Debra is a single parent mom. She has a 14 year old daughter named Casey. The mother complains that Casey is rebelling against her decisions on a regular basis. When Casey comes home she immediately goes into her room and does not come out for hours. Debra has also discovered that Casey has been involved in sexual activity. Debra has caught Casey in quite a few lies over the last several months. Teachers are complaining that Casey seems to be distracted from doing her work. She daydreams through out class time. Casey has also started drinking and doing drugs. This all started when Her dad left her mother for another woman.

1. **Connect the specific characteristics of the problem to the Biblical Framework.**

    a. As you look at the characteristics of the situation/problem are there any expressions of uncaused fleeing being demonstrated? If so, write them down.

    _____
    _____
    _____

    b. As you look at the characteristics of the situation/problem are there any expressions of uncaused fear being demonstrated? If so, write them down.

    _____
    _____
    _____

    c. As you look at the characteristics of the situation/problem are there any expressions of a sense of guilt being demonstrated? If so, write them down.

    _____
    _____
    _____

    d. As you look at the characteristics of the situation/problem are there any secondary unloving/sinful attitudes, words, actions (unloving /sinful attitudes, words or actions being expressed as a result of the main unloving/sinful attitude, word, or action) being demonstrated? If so, write them down.

    _____
    _____
    _____

2. **Identify the Root of the problem. Identify the specific sin (or what we call the lack of love or unloving attitude, word or action towards God or others)**

you believe is producing the sense of guilt, apparently uncaused fear or apparently uncaused fleeing.

    a. Is it an unloving/sinful ***attitude*** producing the sense of guilt, apparently uncaused fear or apparently uncaused fleeing? If so write down what the unloving/sinful attitude is. Write down who or what it is towards.
_____
_____

    b. Is it unloving/sinful ***communication*** producing the sense of guilt, apparently uncaused fear or apparently uncaused fleeing? If so write down what the unloving/sinful communication is. Write down who or what is it towards.
_____
_____

    c. Is it an unloving/sinful ***behavior or lifestyle*** producing the sense of guilt, apparently uncaused fear or apparently uncaused fleeing? If so, write down what the unloving/sinful behavior or lifestyle is.
_____
_____

    d. Is it an unloving/sinful ***way of relating*** producing the sense of guilt, apparently uncaused fear or apparently uncaused fleeing? If so write down what the unloving/sinful way of relating it is. Write down who it is towards?
_____
_____

    e. Is it an unloving/ sinful ***desire*** producing the sense of guilt, apparently uncaused fear or apparently uncaused fleeing? If so write down what the unloving/sinful desire is. Write down who or what it is towards.
_____
_____

3. **Explain the process of moving the person from practicing that specific sin (or what we call a lack of love, or unloving attitude, word or action towards God or others) to expressing love for God and others.**

    a. What are the specific unloving/ sinful issues that need to be confessed?
_____
_____

    b. What do they need to count on being forgiven of by God when they confess?
_____
_____

c. What areas of their life do they need to walk by the Holy Spirit and not carry out the desires of the flesh?

_____
_____

d. As they do this what can they expect from God in this area?

_____
_____

4. **Identify key expressions of love homework assignments you would give to help move the person from practicing the specific sin (or what we call a lack of love, or unloving attitude, word or action towards God or others) to expressing love for God and others. Consider the way you would have them implement these expressions within the context of the problem.**

   a. What expressions of love toward God assignments need to be given in this problem/situation and why?

   _____
   _____
   _____
   _____

   b. What expressions of love towards others assignments need to be given in this problem/situation and why?

   _____
   _____
   _____
   _____

5. **Identify further concepts you need to teach the counselee in order to help them work through their problem and walk in love for God and others.**

   a._____

   b._____

   c._____

   d._____

6. **Think about categories of homework to be used to help implement these concepts.**

    a. *__Hope Homework__* – projects, activities and reading assignments given to help people gain a true hope in Christ in accordance to the problems they are facing

    b. *__Doctrinal Homework__* – projects, activities, and reading assignments given to help people gain a solid theological understanding of their problems so that they can deal with them properly

    c. *__Awareness Homework__* – projects, activities, and reading assignments given to help people become aware of their own sinfulness in the problem so that they can stop deceiving themselves about the problem they are facing and own up to it accordingly

    d. *__Embracing God Homework__* – projects, activities, and reading assignments given to help people to connect with God according to a particular characteristic of God that relates to their problem or sin

    e. *__Action Oriented Homework__* – projects and activities that lead people to put off particular sinful thoughts, desires, conversations, behavior, and lifestyle and to put on particular godly thoughts, desires, conversations, behavior, and lifestyle according to the situation or problem in order to walk in love for God and others

    f. *__Relational Oriented Homework__* – projects and activities that lead people to put off unloving relational patterns and move them to relate in open and loving relational patterns towards others within the situation or problem and abroad

(Concept adapted from *Instruments in a Redeemer's Hand* by Paul Tripp)

Case 25

Daren and Carol have been married for 5 years. They are part of a growing bible church. They are very active members of their Church. Daren and Carol have run into a little trouble. Daren has been struggling with impotence. They have gone to do the doctor and the doctor said that the problem is not medical but mental. Since then Daren has been struggling with masturbation and pornography. He is aroused by those things but when it comes to being with his wife he is easily distracted and struggles with racing thoughts to the point where he becomes impotent. This all started about a few months ago when Carol admitted to having an affair.

1. **Connect the specific characteristics of the problem to the Biblical Framework.**

    a. As you look at the characteristics of the situation/problem are there any expressions of uncaused fleeing being demonstrated? If so, write them down.

    _____
    _____
    _____

    b. As you look at the characteristics of the situation/problem are there any expressions of uncaused fear being demonstrated? If so, write them down.

    _____
    _____
    _____

    c. As you look at the characteristics of the situation/problem are there any expressions of a sense of guilt being demonstrated? If so, write them down.

    _____
    _____
    _____

    d. As you look at the characteristics of the situation/problem are there any secondary unloving/sinful attitudes, words, actions (unloving /sinful attitudes, words or actions being expressed as a result of the main unloving/sinful attitude, word, or action) being demonstrated? If so, write them down.

    _____
    _____
    _____

2. **Identify the Root of the problem. Identify the specific sin (or what we call the lack of love or unloving attitude, word or action towards God or others)**

you believe is producing the sense of guilt, apparently uncaused fear or apparently uncaused fleeing.

    a. Is it an unloving/sinful ***attitude*** producing the sense of guilt, apparently uncaused fear or apparently uncaused fleeing? If so write down what the unloving/sinful attitude is. Write down who or what it is towards.
_____
_____

    b. Is it unloving/sinful ***communication*** producing the sense of guilt, apparently uncaused fear or apparently uncaused fleeing? If so write down what the unloving/sinful communication is. Write down who or what is it towards.
_____
_____

    c. Is it an unloving/sinful ***behavior or lifestyle*** producing the sense of guilt, apparently uncaused fear or apparently uncaused fleeing? If so, write down what the unloving/sinful behavior or lifestyle is.
_____
_____

    d. Is it an unloving/sinful ***way of relating*** producing the sense of guilt, apparently uncaused fear or apparently uncaused fleeing? If so write down what the unloving/sinful way of relating it is. Write down who it is towards?
_____
_____

    e. Is it an unloving/ sinful ***desire*** producing the sense of guilt, apparently uncaused fear or apparently uncaused fleeing? If so write down what the unloving/sinful desire is. Write down who or what it is towards.
_____
_____

3. **Explain the process of moving the person from practicing that specific sin (or what we call a lack of love, or unloving attitude, word or action towards God or others) to expressing love for God and others.**

    a. What are the specific unloving/ sinful issues that need to be confessed?
_____
_____

    b. What do they need to count on being forgiven of by God when they confess?
_____
_____

c. What areas of their life do they need to walk by the Holy Spirit and not carry out the desires of the flesh?

_____
_____

d. As they do this what can they expect from God in this area?

_____
_____

4. **Identify key expressions of love homework assignments you would give to help move the person from practicing the specific sin (or what we call a lack of love, or unloving attitude, word or action towards God or others) to expressing love for God and others. Consider the way you would have them implement these expressions within the context of the problem.**

   a. What expressions of love toward God assignments need to be given in this problem/situation and why?

   _____
   _____
   _____
   _____
   _____

   b. What expressions of love towards others assignments need to be given in this problem/situation and why?

   _____
   _____
   _____
   _____

5. **Identify further concepts you need to teach the counselee in order to help them work through their problem and walk in love for God and others.**

   a. _____

   b. _____

   c. _____

   d. _____

6. **Think about categories of homework to be used to help implement these concepts.**

    a. *Hope Homework* – projects, activities and reading assignments given to help people gain a true hope in Christ in accordance to the problems they are facing

    b. *Doctrinal Homework* – projects, activities, and reading assignments given to help people gain a solid theological understanding of their problems so that they can deal with them properly

    c. *Awareness Homework* – projects, activities, and reading assignments given to help people become aware of their own sinfulness in the problem so that they can stop deceiving themselves about the problem they are facing and own up to it accordingly

    d. *Embracing God Homework* – projects, activities, and reading assignments given to help people to connect with God according to a particular characteristic of God that relates to their problem or sin

    e. *Action Oriented Homework* – projects and activities that lead people to put off particular sinful thoughts, desires, conversations, behavior, and lifestyle and to put on particular godly thoughts, desires, conversations, behavior, and lifestyle according to the situation or problem in order to walk in love for God and others

    f. *Relational Oriented Homework* – projects and activities that lead people to put off unloving relational patterns and move them to relate in open and loving relational patterns towards others within the situation or problem and abroad

(Concept adapted from *Instruments in a Redeemer's Hand* by Paul Tripp)

Case 26

Ralph is 27 years old. He works for a major pharmaceutical company. He is well known and respected within his company. Over the past three weeks right before he is about to go into board meetings he experiences panic attacks. After each board meeting he immediately goes and takes a shower because he believes that the men from mars have been using the power point projector to insert dangerous germs into his body. He is afraid to get on the elevator because the men from mars have placed a wire in the elevator so that they can hear his conversations. He also believes that the President has given secret service men the order to find him and open up his brain. As a result Ralph wears a hat on his head all day. Ralph keeps the blinds in his office closed because he does not want the men from mars to learn what he is thinking as they watch him in the office. This all started three weeks ago after a disagreement between Ralph and his boss. This disagreement almost caused Ralph to lose his job.

1. **Connect the specific characteristics of the problem to the Biblical Framework.**

    a. As you look at the characteristics of the situation/problem are there any expressions of uncaused fleeing being demonstrated? If so, write them down.

    _____
    _____
    _____

    b. As you look at the characteristics of the situation/problem are there any expressions of uncaused fear being demonstrated? If so, write them down.

    _____
    _____
    _____

    c. As you look at the characteristics of the situation/problem are there any expressions of a sense of guilt being demonstrated? If so, write them down.

    _____
    _____
    _____

    d. As you look at the characteristics of the situation/problem are there any secondary unloving/sinful attitudes, words, actions (unloving /sinful attitudes, words or actions being expressed as a result of the main unloving/sinful attitude, word, or action) being demonstrated? If so, write them down.

    _____
    _____

2. **Identify the Root of the problem. Identify the specific sin (or what we call the lack of love or unloving attitude, word or action towards God or others) you believe is producing the sense of guilt, apparently uncaused fear or apparently uncaused fleeing.**

   a. Is it an unloving/sinful ***attitude*** producing the sense of guilt, apparently uncaused fear or apparently uncaused fleeing? If so write down what the unloving/sinful attitude is. Write down who or what it is towards.
   _____
   _____

   b. Is it unloving/sinful ***communication*** producing the sense of guilt, apparently uncaused fear or apparently uncaused fleeing? If so write down what the unloving/sinful communication is. Write down who or what is it towards.
   _____
   _____

   c. Is it an unloving/sinful ***behavior or lifestyle*** producing the sense of guilt, apparently uncaused fear or apparently uncaused fleeing? If so, write down what the unloving/sinful behavior or lifestyle is.
   _____
   _____

   d. Is it an unloving/sinful ***way of relating*** producing the sense of guilt, apparently uncaused fear or apparently uncaused fleeing? If so write down what the unloving/sinful way of relating it is. Write down who it is towards?
   _____
   _____

   e. Is it an unloving/ sinful ***desire*** producing the sense of guilt, apparently uncaused fear or apparently uncaused fleeing? If so write down what the unloving/sinful desire is. Write down who or what it is towards.
   _____
   _____

3. **Explain the process of moving the person from practicing that specific sin (or what we call a lack of love, or unloving attitude, word or action towards God or others) to expressing love for God and others.**

   a. What are the specific unloving/ sinful issues that need to be confessed?
   _____
   _____

   b. What do they need to count on being forgiven of by God when they confess?

c. What areas of their life do they need to walk by the Holy Spirit and not carry out the desires of the flesh?

d. As they do this what can they expect from God in this area?

4. **Identify key expressions of love homework assignments you would give to help move the person from practicing the specific sin (or what we call a lack of love, or unloving attitude, word or action towards God or others) to expressing love for God and others. Consider the way you would have them implement these expressions within the context of the problem.**

   a. What expressions of love toward God assignments need to be given in this problem/situation and why?

   b. What expressions of love towards others assignments need to be given in this problem/situation and why?

5. **Identify further concepts you need to teach the counselee in order to help them work through their problem and walk in love for God and others.**

   a.

   b.

   c.

   d.

6. **Think about categories of homework to be used to help implement these concepts.**

    a. *__Hope Homework__* – projects, activities and reading assignments given to help people gain a true hope in Christ in accordance to the problems they are facing

    b. *__Doctrinal Homework__* – projects, activities, and reading assignments given to help people gain a solid theological understanding of their problems so that they can deal with them properly

    c. *__Awareness Homework__* – projects, activities, and reading assignments given to help people become aware of their own sinfulness in the problem so that they can stop deceiving themselves about the problem they are facing and own up to it accordingly

    d. *__Embracing God Homework__* – projects, activities, and reading assignments given to help people to connect with God according to a particular characteristic of God that relates to their problem or sin

    e. *__Action Oriented Homework__* – projects and activities that lead people to put off particular sinful thoughts, desires, conversations, behavior, and lifestyle and to put on particular godly thoughts, desires, conversations, behavior, and lifestyle according to the situation or problem in order to walk in love for God and others

    f. *__Relational Oriented Homework__* – projects and activities that lead people to put off unloving relational patterns and move them to relate in open and loving relational patterns towards others within the situation or problem and abroad

(Concept adapted from *Instruments in a Redeemer's Hand* by Paul Tripp)

Case 27

Katie is 35 years old. She has been married to John for about 4 years. Katie and John have a good marriage. Every year when they go to visit John's family Katie experiences a lot of restlessness. She also complains of muscle tension and starts to get very irritable the closer they get to his parent's house. When Katie seeks to communicate with John's mother she forgets his mother's name. When the family wants to go out and do activities Katie complains of fatigue and loss of energy and stays in the house. Katie finds it hard to sleep in the house at night so she just stays up most of the night and watches TV. This was not always the case. This started last year. Katie overheard John's mother telling John that she did not like Katie and wished He would have married someone else.

1. **Connect the specific characteristics of the problem to the Biblical Framework.**

   a. As you look at the characteristics of the situation/problem are there any expressions of uncaused fleeing being demonstrated? If so, write them down.

   _____
   _____
   _____

   b. As you look at the characteristics of the situation/problem are there any expressions of uncaused fear being demonstrated? If so, write them down.

   _____
   _____
   _____

   c. As you look at the characteristics of the situation/problem are there any expressions of a sense of guilt being demonstrated? If so, write them down.

   _____
   _____
   _____

   d. As you look at the characteristics of the situation/problem are there any secondary unloving/sinful attitudes, words, actions (unloving /sinful attitudes, words or actions being expressed as a result of the main unloving/sinful attitude, word, or action) being demonstrated? If so, write them down.

   _____
   _____
   _____

2. **Identify the Root of the problem. Identify the specific sin (or what we call the lack of love or unloving attitude, word or action towards God or others) you believe is producing the sense of guilt, apparently uncaused fear or apparently uncaused fleeing.**

   a. Is it an unloving/sinful ***attitude*** producing the sense of guilt, apparently uncaused fear or apparently uncaused fleeing? If so write down what the unloving/sinful attitude is. Write down who or what it is towards.

   _____
   _____

   b. Is it unloving/sinful ***communication*** producing the sense of guilt, apparently uncaused fear or apparently uncaused fleeing? If so write down what the unloving/sinful communication is. Write down who or what is it towards.

   _____
   _____

   c. Is it an unloving/sinful ***behavior or lifestyle*** producing the sense of guilt, apparently uncaused fear or apparently uncaused fleeing? If so, write down what the unloving/sinful behavior or lifestyle is.

   _____
   _____

   d. Is it an unloving/sinful ***way of relating*** producing the sense of guilt, apparently uncaused fear or apparently uncaused fleeing? If so write down what the unloving/sinful way of relating it is. Write down who it is towards?

   _____
   _____

   e. Is it an unloving/ sinful ***desire*** producing the sense of guilt, apparently uncaused fear or apparently uncaused fleeing? If so write down what the unloving/sinful desire is. Write down who or what it is towards.

   _____
   _____

3. **Explain the process of moving the person from practicing that specific sin (or what we call a lack of love, or unloving attitude, word or action towards God or others) to expressing love for God and others.**

   a. What are the specific unloving/ sinful issues that need to be confessed?

   _____
   _____

b. What do they need to count on being forgiven of by God when they confess?
_____
_____

c. What areas of their life do they need to walk by the Holy Spirit and not carry out the desires of the flesh?
_____
_____

d. As they do this what can they expect from God in this area?
_____
_____

4. **Identify key expressions of love homework assignments you would give to help move the person from practicing the specific sin (or what we call a lack of love, or unloving attitude, word or action towards God or others) to expressing love for God and others. Consider the way you would have them implement these expressions within the context of the problem.**

   a. What expressions of love toward God assignments need to be given in this problem/situation and why?
   _____
   _____
   _____
   _____

   b. What expressions of love towards others assignments need to be given in this problem/situation and why?
   _____
   _____
   _____
   _____

5. **Identify further concepts you need to teach the counselee in order to help them work through their problem and walk in love for God and others.**

   a._____

   b._____

   c._____

   d._____

6. **Think about categories of homework to be used to help implement these concepts.**

    a. *Hope Homework* – projects, activities and reading assignments given to help people gain a true hope in Christ in accordance to the problems they are facing

    b. *Doctrinal Homework* – projects, activities, and reading assignments given to help people gain a solid theological understanding of their problems so that they can deal with them properly

    c. *Awareness Homework* – projects, activities, and reading assignments given to help people become aware of their own sinfulness in the problem so that they can stop deceiving themselves about the problem they are facing and own up to it accordingly

    d. *Embracing God Homework* – projects, activities, and reading assignments given to help people to connect with God according to a particular characteristic of God that relates to their problem or sin

    e. *Action Oriented Homework* – projects and activities that lead people to put off particular sinful thoughts, desires, conversations, behavior, and lifestyle and to put on particular godly thoughts, desires, conversations, behavior, and lifestyle according to the situation or problem in order to walk in love for God and others

    f. *Relational Oriented Homework* – projects and activities that lead people to put off unloving relational patterns and move them to relate in open and loving relational patterns towards others within the situation or problem and abroad

(Concept adapted from *Instruments in a Redeemer's Hand* by Paul Tripp)

Case 28

Karen is concerned about her husband Ted. Ted will not interact with his friends or family. He will not eat. He has lost over 15 pounds in the last 3 weeks. He talks about suicide on a daily basis. Ted talks about how empty he feels and wishes that his empty feelings would go away. He has called in sick and has taken a three month leave of absence from his job. He complains of anxiety and fears and that his time of death is coming soon. This all started when Ted's best friend died in a car accident as Ted was driving the car.

1. **Connect the specific characteristics of the problem to the Biblical Framework.**

    a. As you look at the characteristics of the situation/problem are there any expressions of uncaused fleeing being demonstrated? If so, write them down.

    _____
    _____
    _____

    b. As you look at the characteristics of the situation/problem are there any expressions of uncaused fear being demonstrated? If so, write them down.

    _____
    _____
    _____

    c. As you look at the characteristics of the situation/problem are there any expressions of a sense of guilt being demonstrated? If so, write them down.

    _____
    _____
    _____

    d. As you look at the characteristics of the situation/problem are there any secondary unloving/sinful attitudes, words, actions (unloving /sinful attitudes, words or actions being expressed as a result of the main unloving/sinful attitude, word, or action) being demonstrated? If so, write them down.

    _____
    _____
    _____

2. **Identify the Root of the problem. Identify the specific sin (or what we call the lack of love or unloving attitude, word or action towards God or others) you believe is producing the sense of guilt, apparently uncaused fear or apparently uncaused fleeing.**

a. Is it an unloving/sinful ***attitude*** producing the sense of guilt, apparently uncaused fear or apparently uncaused fleeing? If so write down what the unloving/sinful attitude is. Write down who or what it is towards.
___
___

b. Is it unloving/sinful ***communication*** producing the sense of guilt, apparently uncaused fear or apparently uncaused fleeing? If so write down what the unloving/sinful communication is. Write down who or what is it towards.
___
___

c. Is it an unloving/sinful ***behavior or lifestyle*** producing the sense of guilt, apparently uncaused fear or apparently uncaused fleeing? If so, write down what the unloving/sinful behavior or lifestyle is.
___
___

d. Is it an unloving/sinful ***way of relating*** producing the sense of guilt, apparently uncaused fear or apparently uncaused fleeing? If so write down what the unloving/sinful way of relating it is. Write down who it is towards?
___
___

e. Is it an unloving/sinful ***desire*** producing the sense of guilt, apparently uncaused fear or apparently uncaused fleeing? If so write down what the unloving/sinful desire is. Write down who or what it is towards.
___
___

3. **Explain the process of moving the person from practicing that specific sin (or what we call a lack of love, or unloving attitude, word or action towards God or others) to expressing love for God and others.**

    a. What are the specific unloving/ sinful issues that need to be confessed?
    ___
    ___

    b. What do they need to count on being forgiven of by God when they confess?
    ___
    ___

c. What areas of their life do they need to walk by the Holy Spirit and not carry out the desires of the flesh?

d. As they do this what can they expect from God in this area?

4. **Identify key expressions of love homework assignments you would give to help move the person from practicing the specific sin (or what we call a lack of love, or unloving attitude, word or action towards God or others) to expressing love for God and others . Consider the way you would have them implement these expressions within the context of the problem.**

   a. What expressions of love toward God assignments need to be given in this problem/situation and why?

   b. What expressions of love towards others assignments need to be given in this problem/situation and why?

5. **Identify further concepts you need to teach the counselee in order to help them work through their problem and walk in love for God and others.**

   a. _____

   b. _____

   c. _____

   d. _____

6. **Think about categories of homework to be used to help implement these concepts.**

    a. *__Hope Homework__* – projects, activities and reading assignments given to help people gain a true hope in Christ in accordance to the problems they are facing

    b. *__Doctrinal Homework__* – projects, activities, and reading assignments given to help people gain a solid theological understanding of their problems so that they can deal with them properly

    c. *__Awareness Homework__* – projects, activities, and reading assignments given to help people become aware of their own sinfulness in the problem so that they can stop deceiving themselves about the problem they are facing and own up to it accordingly

    d. *__Embracing God Homework__* – projects, activities, and reading assignments given to help people to connect with God according to a particular characteristic of God that relates to their problem or sin

    e. *__Action Oriented Homework__* – projects and activities that lead people to put off particular sinful thoughts, desires, conversations, behavior, and lifestyle and to put on particular godly thoughts, desires, conversations, behavior, and lifestyle according to the situation or problem in order to walk in love for God and others

    f. *__Relational Oriented Homework__* – projects and activities that lead people to put off unloving relational patterns and move them to relate in open and loving relational patterns towards others within the situation or problem and abroad

(Concept adapted from *Instruments in a Redeemer's Hand* by Paul Tripp)

Case 29

Phillip is 24 years old. He lives with his parents. Phillip has not been able to sleep at night. He has been down on himself for the last three weeks. He has been experiencing panic attacks whenever he is alone. He tends to pour himself into video games when the panic attacks happen. He also has been eating a lot food when he is alone. He has been withdrawing and not communicating to any of his friends. This has been happening ever since his parents have been arguing and threatening to divorce.

1. **Connect the specific characteristics of the problem to the Biblical Framework.**

    a. As you look at the characteristics of the situation/problem are there any expressions of uncaused fleeing being demonstrated? If so, write them down.
    _____
    _____
    _____

    b. As you look at the characteristics of the situation/problem are there any expressions of uncaused fear being demonstrated? If so, write them down.
    _____
    _____
    _____

    c. As you look at the characteristics of the situation/problem are there any expressions of a sense of guilt being demonstrated? If so, write them down.
    _____
    _____
    _____

    d. As you look at the characteristics of the situation/problem are there any secondary unloving/sinful attitudes, words, actions (unloving /sinful attitudes, words or actions being expressed as a result of the main unloving/sinful attitude, word, or action) being demonstrated? If so, write them down.
    _____
    _____
    _____

2. **Identify the Root of the problem. Identify the specific sin (or what we call the lack of love or unloving attitude, word or action towards God or others)**

you believe is producing the sense of guilt, apparently uncaused fear or apparently uncaused fleeing.

   a. Is it an unloving/sinful ***attitude*** producing the sense of guilt, apparently uncaused fear or apparently uncaused fleeing? If so write down what the unloving/sinful attitude is. Write down who or what it is towards.
   _____
   _____

   b. Is it unloving/sinful ***communication*** producing the sense of guilt, apparently uncaused fear or apparently uncaused fleeing? If so write down what the unloving/sinful communication is. Write down who or what is it towards.
   _____
   _____

   c. Is it an unloving/sinful ***behavior or lifestyle*** producing the sense of guilt, apparently uncaused fear or apparently uncaused fleeing? If so, write down what the unloving/sinful behavior or lifestyle is.
   _____
   _____

   d. Is it an unloving/sinful ***way of relating*** producing the sense of guilt, apparently uncaused fear or apparently uncaused fleeing? If so write down what the unloving/sinful way of relating it is. Write down who it is towards?
   _____
   _____

   e. Is it an unloving/ sinful ***desire*** producing the sense of guilt, apparently uncaused fear or apparently uncaused fleeing? If so write down what the unloving/sinful desire is. Write down who or what it is towards.
   _____
   _____

3. **Explain the process of moving the person from practicing that specific sin (or what we call a lack of love, or unloving attitude, word or action towards God or others) to expressing love for God and others.**

   a. What are the specific unloving/ sinful issues that need to be confessed?
   _____
   _____

   b. What do they need to count on being forgiven of by God when they confess?
   _____
   _____

c. What areas of their life do they need to walk by the Holy Spirit and not carry out the desires of the flesh?

_____
_____

d. As they do this what can they expect from God in this area?

_____
_____

4. **Identify key expressions of love homework assignments you would give to help move the person from practicing the specific sin (or what we call a lack of love, or unloving attitude, word or action towards God or others) to expressing love for God and others. Consider the way you would have them implement these expressions within the context of the problem.**

   a. What expressions of love toward God assignments need to be given in this problem/situation and why?

   _____
   _____
   _____
   _____
   _____

   b. What expressions of love towards others assignments need to be given in this problem/situation and why?

   _____
   _____
   _____
   _____

5. **Identify further concepts you need to teach the counselee in order to help them work through their problem and walk in love for God and others.**

   a. _____

   b. _____

   c. _____

   d. _____

6. **Think about categories of homework to be used to help implement these concepts.**

    a. *Hope Homework* – projects, activities and reading assignments given to help people gain a true hope in Christ in accordance to the problems they are facing

    b. *Doctrinal Homework* – projects, activities, and reading assignments given to help people gain a solid theological understanding of their problems so that they can deal with them properly

    c. *Awareness Homework* – projects, activities, and reading assignments given to help people become aware of their own sinfulness in the problem so that they can stop deceiving themselves about the problem they are facing and own up to it accordingly

    d. *Embracing God Homework* – projects, activities, and reading assignments given to help people to connect with God according to a particular characteristic of God that relates to their problem or sin

    e. *Action Oriented Homework* – projects and activities that lead people to put off particular sinful thoughts, desires, conversations, behavior, and lifestyle and to put on particular godly thoughts, desires, conversations, behavior, and lifestyle according to the situation or problem in order to walk in love for God and others

    f. *Relational Oriented Homework* – projects and activities that lead people to put off unloving relational patterns and move them to relate in open and loving relational patterns towards others within the situation or problem and abroad

(Concept adapted from *Instruments in a Redeemer's Hand* by Paul Tripp)

Case 30

Olsen is a 40 year old male. Olsen works for a meat company. Lately Olsen has been withdrawing from co-workers, wife, and friends. He talks about suicide and finds it hard to go to sleep at night. Olsen will spend hours watching TV and staring into space. He complains of fearful dreams. This started around the time Olsen find out he had cancer.

1. **Connect the specific characteristics of the problem to the Biblical Framework.**

   a. As you look at the characteristics of the situation/problem are there any expressions of uncaused fleeing being demonstrated? If so, write them down.
   _____
   _____
   _____

   b. As you look at the characteristics of the situation/problem are there any expressions of uncaused fear being demonstrated? If so, write them down.
   _____
   _____
   _____

   c. As you look at the characteristics of the situation/problem are there any expressions of a sense of guilt being demonstrated? If so, write them down.
   _____
   _____
   _____

   d. As you look at the characteristics of the situation/problem are there any secondary unloving/sinful attitudes, words, actions (unloving /sinful attitudes, words or actions being expressed as a result of the main unloving/sinful attitude, word, or action) being demonstrated? If so, write them down.
   _____
   _____
   _____

2. **Identify the Root of the problem. Identify the specific sin (or what we call the lack of love or unloving attitude, word or action towards God or others) you believe is producing the sense of guilt, apparently uncaused fear or apparently uncaused fleeing.**

a. Is it an unloving/sinful ***attitude*** producing the sense of guilt, apparently uncaused fear or apparently uncaused fleeing? If so write down what the unloving/sinful attitude is. Write down who or what it is towards.

___

b. Is it unloving/sinful ***communication*** producing the sense of guilt, apparently uncaused fear or apparently uncaused fleeing? If so write down what the unloving/sinful communication is. Write down who or what is it towards.

___

c. Is it an unloving/sinful ***behavior or lifestyle*** producing the sense of guilt, apparently uncaused fear or apparently uncaused fleeing? If so, write down what the unloving/sinful behavior or lifestyle is.

___

d. Is it an unloving/sinful ***way of relating*** producing the sense of guilt, apparently uncaused fear or apparently uncaused fleeing? If so write down what the unloving/sinful way of relating it is. Write down who it is towards?

___

e. Is it an unloving/ sinful ***desire*** producing the sense of guilt, apparently uncaused fear or apparently uncaused fleeing? If so write down what the unloving/sinful desire is. Write down who or what it is towards.

___

3. **Explain the process of moving the person from practicing that specific sin (or what we call a lack of love, or unloving attitude, word or action towards God or others) to expressing love for God and others.**

   a. What are the specific unloving/ sinful issues that need to be confessed?

   ___

   b. What do they need to count on being forgiven of by God when they confess?

   ___

c. What areas of their life do they need to walk by the Holy Spirit and not carry out the desires of the flesh?

_____
_____

d. As they do this what can they expect from God in this area?

_____
_____

4. **Identify key expressions of love homework assignments you would give to help move the person from practicing the specific sin (or what we call a lack of love, or unloving attitude, word or action towards God or others) to expressing love for God and others . Consider the way you would have them implement these expressions within the context of the problem.**

   a. What expressions of love toward God assignments need to be given in this problem/situation and why?

   _____
   _____
   _____
   _____
   _____

   b. What expressions of love towards others assignments need to be given in this problem/situation and why?

   _____
   _____
   _____
   _____

5. **Identify further concepts you need to teach the counselee in order to help them work through their problem and walk in love for God and others.**

   a. _____

   b. _____

   c. _____

   d. _____

6. **Think about categories of homework to be used to help implement these concepts.**

   a. ***Hope Homework*** – projects, activities and reading assignments given to help people gain a true hope in Christ in accordance to the problems they are facing

   b. ***Doctrinal Homework*** – projects, activities, and reading assignments given to help people gain a solid theological understanding of their problems so that they can deal with them properly

   c. ***Awareness Homework*** – projects, activities, and reading assignments given to help people become aware of their own sinfulness in the problem so that they can stop deceiving themselves about the problem they are facing and own up to it accordingly

   d. ***Embracing God Homework*** – projects, activities, and reading assignments given to help people to connect with God according to a particular characteristic of God that relates to their problem or sin

   e. ***Action Oriented Homework*** – projects and activities that lead people to put off particular sinful thoughts, desires, conversations, behavior, and lifestyle and to put on particular godly thoughts, desires, conversations, behavior, and lifestyle according to the situation or problem in order to walk in love for God and others

   f. ***Relational Oriented Homework*** – projects and activities that lead people to put off unloving relational patterns and move them to relate in open and loving relational patterns towards others within the situation or problem and abroad

(Concept adapted from *Instruments in a Redeemer's Hand* by Paul Tripp)

Appendix

Biblical Counseling and Spiritual Life

A. God is saving souls from the power, penalty, and soon the presence of sin (Ephesians 2:1-10, Colossians 1:12-14).

B. God is maturing saints into the image of Jesus Christ (2Corinthains 3:18, Romans 8:29-30).

C. God is using the Church through evangelism to save souls (2Corinthians 5:18-20, Colossians 1:3-6).

D. God is using the Church through discipleship to mature saints into the image of Christ (Matthew 28:18-20, Ephesians 4:11-15).

E. Biblical Counseling is an avenue whereby evangelism and discipleship can take place resulting in God using it to save a soul from the power, penalty and soon presence of sin and maturing saints into the image of Jesus Christ.

F. All Biblical Counseling should be built around three key objectives:

1. To lead a person into salvation (2Corinthains 5:11-21)

2. To lead Christians into putting off particular sinful habits that keep them from walking in love toward God and others (Galatians 6:1)

3. To lead Christians into putting on loving attitudes and actions towards God and others leading them to become like Christ in all things (Ephesians 4:11-32)

G. Those who belong to Christ must pursue spiritual maturity in Christ. In order to grow to spiritual maturity in Jesus Christ, it is necessary for you to know and operate in the *biblical process of change*. As God is working inside of you (Philippians 2:12), you are to respond accordingly (Philippians 2:13). Here is an example of how it works (2Timothy 3:16-17):

1. **Teaching Stage**: The Holy Spirit guides, convicts and enlightens your mind through the Word of God, the Body of Christ, circumstances, and prayer (John

16:8-13, 1Corinthians 2:9-12, Hebrews 4:12, 1John 4:4-6, 1Peter 4:12-13, Romans 8:26-27).

2. **Conviction Stage:** God begins to focus your attention in particular areas of life convincing you that change is necessary. (Phil. 3:14-15, 2Cor. 7:10-11).

3. **Correction Stage:** You make a decision to abandon a sin issue and begin a new thought, word, or action trusting God's power to make things function accordingly (2Corinthians 7:10-11, Proverbs 28:13-14).

4. **Training Stage:** As you are responding to God's conviction you are seeking to put to practice what God has commanded in His Word.

    a. The power of God you are walking in harmony with God in areas where you were once disobedient.
    b. You are experiencing victory: a deeper fellowship with God and with others (2Peter 1:1-11, Proverbs 12:13, 24:16, John 8:31-32, Luke 8:4-18, Ephesians 4:11-13, 1John 3:1-3).
    (Concept adapted from Jay Adams)

H. Biblical Counselors can help lead counselees through each stage by:

1. helping counselees look closely at and work hard on having a thought life that is leasing to God as God's Word commands (Romans 12:2-3)

2. helping counselees look closely at work hard on communicating in ways that are honest and edifying to others as God's Word commands (Ephesians 4:29)

3. helping counselees look closely at and work hard on walking in behavior that is consistent with Christ's Character as God's Word commands (Ephesians 5:1-17)

4. helping counselees look closely at and work hard on relating to others in ways that demonstrate the love of Christ as God's Word commands (Romans 13:8-12)

5. helping counselees look closely at and work hard on serving others in ways that will bear their burdens and meet their needs as God's Word commands (1Peter 4:10)

6. helping counselees look closely at and work hard on living a holy and sacrificial life unto Jesus Christ as God's Word commands (Galatians 5:16-24)

I. There are six key categories of homework that can be given to guide counselees into the process of change according the stage of change they may be in and according to the area of their lives where change may need to take place. This is to lead them into escaping the corruption of their flesh, the world and the devil unto spiritual maturity in Jesus Christ:

1. ***Hope Homework*** – projects, activities and reading assignments given to help people gain a true hope in Christ in accordance to the problems they are facing

2. ***Doctrinal Homework*** – projects, activities, and reading assignments given to help people gain a solid theological understanding of their problems so that they can deal with them properly

3. ***Awareness Homework*** – projects, activities, and reading assignments given to help people become aware of their own sinfulness in the problem so that they can stop receiving themselves about the problem they are facing and own up to it accordingly

4. ***Embracing God Homework*** – projects, activities, and reading assignments given to help people to connect with God according to a particular characteristic of God that relates to their problem or sin

5. ***Action Oriented Homework*** – projects and activities that lead people to put off particular sinful thoughts, desires, conversations, behavior, and lifestyle and to put on particular godly thoughts, desires, conversations, behavior, and lifestyle according to the situation or problem

6. ***Relational Oriented Homework*** – projects and activities that lead people to put off unloving relational patterns and move them to relate in open and loving relational patterns towards others within the situation or problem and abroad

(Portions of this information was adapted from *Instruments in a Redeemer's Hand* by Paul Tripp)

J. As a counselor determines the category of homework to be given, he can use various methods of implementation to help move counselees into to the process of change resulting in escaping the corruption of their flesh, the world and the devil unto spiritual maturity in Jesus Christ. Some of those methods of implementation are:

1. ***Scripture reading*** – leading the counselee into seeing and discovering the reality of God's Word in accordance to their problem; to lead them into a consistent pattern of reading and studying God's Word to understand the nature of it and to live by the content in it in order that they may know God intimately and to be useful to Him practically (Concept adapted from Randy Patten)

2. ***Literature reading*** – leading the counselee into reading various biblical literature that shows them how to evaluate and address the problem from God's standpoint in a comprehensive manner so that they may turn from it and walk in obedience to God accordingly (Concept adapted from Randy Patten)

3. ***Scripture Memorization*** – leading the counselee into memorizing Scripture so that they may be transformed in their thinking and turn away from sin unto living as God has commanded (Concept adapted from Randy Patten)

4. ***Prayer*** – leading the counselee into the process of prayer so they may learn how to communicate with God in a way that will lead them into genuine fellowship with God; so they my learn how to make request for others and themselves in an appropriate manner (Concept adapted from Randy Patten)

5. ***Projects*** – activities that lead the counselee into stopping some thought, word or action or leading them into starting some thought, word, or action in relation to God, others, self or circumstances as it relates to the issues brought up in the counseling sessions (Concept adapted from Randy Patten)

6. ***Log Lists/Journals*** – having the counselee to write down specific thoughts, behaviors, actions or words to evaluate where change has taken place or to see where change needs to take place

7. **Church Participation** – leading the counselee into:

    a. *Membership* – the counselee would be lead to join a local church that they may experience love and enjoy the blessings of God-honoring relationships.

    b. *Maturity* – the counselee would be lead to get involved in discipleship courses in a local Church that would lead them into loving God, loving others on a consistent basis and living a life that reflects the character of Christ

    c. *Magnification* – the counselee would be led to come to appreciate value and adore the character of God through heart-felt genuine worship of Him in a local Church.

    d. *Ministry* – the counselee would be led to join a ministry where they can develop in bearing burdens and meeting needs according to the various relationships they will develop through the local Church

    e. *Missions* – the counselee would be led into supporting a local Church in sharing and defending the Christian faith

K. There are four basic personalities you may run into when involved in biblical counseling:

1. Those who *lack knowledge* yet once they receive it are able to work on their problems and honor God.

2. Those who *have knowledge* but refuse to apply what they know to work on their problems and honor God.

3. Those who *have knowledge* but don't know how to apply it to their problems and honor God.

4. Those who *lack knowledge* and are not interested in getting knowledge to work on their problems and honor God.

(Adapted from the various teachings of Jay Adams)

L. As counselors evaluate what counselees need, they can give the right kind of homework in the right area to help counselees move through the process of change to spiritual maturity in Jesus Christ resulting in:

1. Counselees evaluating things from a biblical perspective (Psalm 1:1-3, James 3:13-17).

2. Counselees reflecting the lifestyle of Christ consistently (Galatians 5:16-23, 2Peter 1:1-10).

3. Counselees experiencing an intimacy with God that goes beyond intellectual knowledge (John 8:31-32, John 14:21, Ephesians 3:14-20).

4. Counselees sharing the Gospel consistently (2Corinthians 5:11-20)

5. Counselees defending the Gospel consistently (1Peter 3:15, 2Timothy 2:24-26).

6. Counselees serving others through their gift(s) producing positive results (1Peter 4:10-11, John 15:1-5, Luke 6:43-45).

(concept adapted from Wilford Darden.)

Progressive Sanctification and Homework Assignments

The Areas of Change	The Process of Change	The Homework to help implement the process of Change	The Activities to help implement the homework	The Examples of Implementation of activities
Thoughts and Attitudes	Realize our Sin	Hope Homework	Scripture Reading	Reading particular Books of the Bible that connect to your issues
Intentions and Desires	Remorse over our Sin	Theological Homework	Literature Reading	Reading literature that addresses your issues
Conversation and Communication	Renounce our Sin	Awareness Homework	Scripture Memorization	Memorizing and Meditating on Scripture/ Biblical Concepts according to your issues
Behavior and Lifestyle	Repent of our Sin	Embracing God Homework	Prayer	Writing out Log list, or journals to evaluate yourself or your progress
Relational Patterns	Renew our Minds	Action Oriented Homework	Projects	Communicating certain things to God or people on a regular basis
Service for God and Others	Replace our Sin with the right thing to do in the areas	Relation Oriented Homework	Log List/ Journals/ Church Participation	Practicing certain attitudes, actions or behaviors towards God, others, and in situations/ Getting involved in particular aspects of Church life to enhance growth into the image of Christ

Key Points to Consider For Biblical Change

1. **The Premise of Biblical Change**
    a. To establish a right relationship with God the Father through our Lord Jesus Christ
    b. To put off particular sins that keep us from loving God and loving others
    c. To put on particular loving attitudes and actions towards God and others that lead us to become like Christ in all things

2. **The Places Where Biblical Change will have to take place**
    a. People will need to change in thoughts, attitudes, motives, and desires
    b. People will need to change in conversations and communication
    c. People will need to change in behavior and lifestyle
    d. People will need to change in how they relate to others
    e. People will need to change in the way the serve God and others

3. **The Parameters of Biblical Change**
    a. People will need gain a biblical understanding of God and submit to His will accordingly
    b. People will need to gain a biblical understanding of themselves and submit to God's will accordingly
    c. People will need to gain a biblical understanding of others and submit to God's will accordingly
    d. People will need to gain a biblical understand of life's situations and circumstances and submit to God's will accordingly

4. **The Process of Biblical Change (all empowered by the Holy Spirit)**
    a. Renouncing of sin (1John 1:9, James 5:16)
    b. Repenting of sin (2Corinthians 7:10-11, Proverbs 28:13)
    c. Replacement of sin with love for God through obedience in the area of the sin (Ephesians 4:22-24, Colossians 3:1-17)
    d. Replacement of sin with love for others through doing what is right to and for them accordingly (Ephesians 4: 22-24, Colossians 3:1-17)

Key Concepts to Teach Your Counselee in order to Lead Him into Biblical Change

Concept I – Teach the Counselee the Gospel of Jesus Christ	
• Teach him who is Jesus Christ. • The doctrine of salvation	• The way of salvation • The marks of salvation (Bullet points adapted from Randall D. Westerberg from a paper "The Lack of Assurance of Salvation"; Doctorate of Ministry Paper for Southern Baptist Theological Seminary)
Concept II – Teach the Counselee what He can and cannot control	
• Teach him to distinguish between what he is concerned about and what he is responsible for. • Help him understand how not making the distinction can create complications resulting him negating his responsibilities by being consumed with what he is concerned about but cannot control • Help him understand that he cannot control what people think, say, or do • Help understand that he cannot control the outcome of events	• Teach him that he can control what he thinks, says, does • Help him understand that he is motivated either by selfish desires or love for God in relation to People and situations • Help him understand that the condition of his life is a by-product of heart choices not the actions of others or circumstances in life
Concept III – Teach the Counselee the Two Basic Choices in Life (to live for God or to live for self)	
• Teach him that he is either love oriented or pleasure oriented • Teach him that his choices are driven by his thoughts • Teach him that at core of his thoughts is either the love of self and the love of pleasure or the love of God and the love of others	• Help him understand that if he consumed with the love of pleasure and love of self he may create idols of the heart and bring destruction to his life as a result • Teach him the steps to turn from this all ways he may be turning away from God
Concept IV – Teach the Counselee The Biblical Framework	
• Help him understand that our ambition in life is to please God • Help him understand that God has given two basic commandments to please Him. (Love God and Love His Neighbor) • Teach him that God has set up consequences within our hearts to happen when we don't walk in love for God and love for others • Teach him that God has set up consequences within our hearts to happen when we walk in love for God and love for others	• Help him learn and understand the principle and picture of a sense of guilt, apparently uncaused fear, and apparently uncaused fleeing as the consequences of not walking in love for God and others • Help him learn and understand the principle and picture of the peace of God, confidence before God and drawing near to God as the consequences of walking in love for God and others • Help him learn understand the process of moving from a lack of love for God and others to love for God and others

Concept V – Teach the Counselee the Biblical Precept of Love

- Teach him basic categories of Love
- Teach him the calling to Agape Love
- Teach him the characteristics of agape love
- Help him understand how it applies to his life

Concept VI – Teach the Counselee the Four Kinds of Human Relationships

- Explain the principle of being open and unloving
- Explain the principle of being closed and loving
- Explain the principle of being open and loving
- Explain the principle of being closed and unloving
- Help him understand how it applies to his life

Concept VII – Teach the Counselee the Basic Process of Change (Progressive Sanctification)

- Explain the practice of confessing sin
- Explain the practice of repenting of sin
- Explain the practice of radical amputation of sin
- Explain the practice of replacing sin with love for God and others in the specific area where sin is being practiced
- Explain the importance this being life-style not an event

Concept VIII – Teach the Counselee the Danger of Fearing Man above Fearing God

- Explain the definition of the fear of man
- Explain what we fear of man
- Explain why we fear man
- Give specific exercises to help him to overcome the fear of man

Concept IV – Teach the Counselee a Biblical View of Anger

- Give a biblical definition of anger
- Explain the two types of anger
- Teach the issues that lead to anger
- Teach the sources of anger
- Give biblical solutions for anger

Concept X – Teach the Counselee a Biblical View of Self-Esteem, Self Image, and Self Love

- Give a definition of Self-Esteem, Self Image, and Self Love
- Explain the difference between them
- Show the counselee how it applies to his life

Concept XI – Teach the Counselee how to organize his life around a Christ-Centered Agenda

- Teach and explain a Biblical View of God and His agenda
- Help him lay out a mission plan for his life and family according to God's agenda
- Help him identify the God-given roles and responsibilities for himself and family and write out a job descriptions of each according to Scripture
- Help him organize his life around these particular roles and responsibilities in way that is God-honoring

Concept XII – Teach the Counselee The Four "P"S along with Conflict Resolution Skills

- Teach and explain how *Perceptions* lead you see people and circumstances according to your own agenda overlooking God's perspective
- Teach and explain how *Preferences* lead you to focus on your way of things being done with people and situation above considering others
- Teach and explain how *Pain* from the disappointment of being let down by others may keep you consumed with self above considering others
- Teach and explain how *Passion* for your own self interest may keep you inconsiderate of others

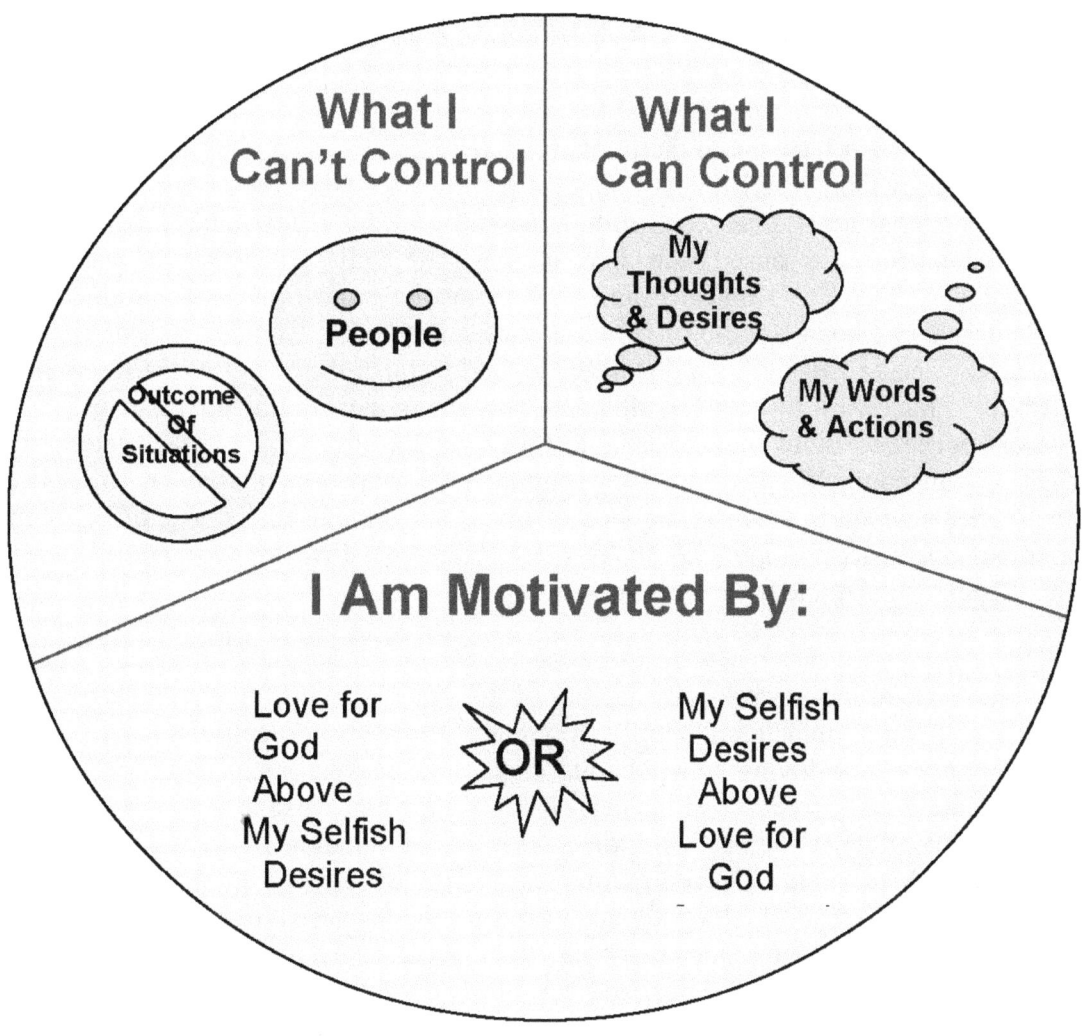

What I Can and Can't Control in Life

      We cannot control people or the outcome of situations. We can only control our own thoughts, desires, words, and actions. Therefore, we need to evaluate and take responsibility for how we are responding to people and the outcome of situations. We need to evaluate what is motivating us with people and the outcome of situations. Are we motivated by love for God above our selfish desires? Or, are we motivated by our selfish desires above love for God?

What Is The Biblical Framework?

It is a picture of what happens in the immaterial heart of man as a result of his choice to obey or to disobey God. The Biblical Framework shows how the conscience produces in a person's immaterial heart a sense of guilt, apparently uncaused fear, and a desire to flee from the apparently uncaused fear and a sense of guilt when he is walking in disobedience to God. The Biblical Framework shows how the conscience produces in a person's immaterial heart a sense of peace, a confidence before God and a desire to draw near to God when he is walking in obedience to God through the power of the Holy Spirit. The Biblical Framework reveals that all sin is basically demonstrating a lack love for God and others. Since the Bible commands us to love God and love others (which are the two greatest commandments) any sin we commit is a direct violation of these two commandments which in essence is a lack of love for God and others. Therefore, proper response of obedience to God's commands demonstrates a love for God and a love for others. Listen to this quote from Rich Thomson:

> The Biblical Framework is a diagram of the inner workings of the human heart (man's immaterial being). It pictures how man's conscience, in response to the loving and unloving choices he makes, instinctively and instantaneously produces in his heart a knowledge and sense of peace or of guilt, confidence before God or a fear of His judgment (apparently uncaused fear), and a desire to draw near to Him or to flee from that sense of guilt and fear of His judgment (apparently uncaused fleeing).These conscience-stimulated inner reactions, then, drive many of man's deepest thoughts, motivations, desires, and emotions – both those that are loving, open, and beneficial and those that are unloving, detrimental, and/or hidden in unexplained fears (or anxieties), obscure choices, and irrational behaviors. Beneficial or detrimental to both man's immaterial being and to his physiology.

(Information adapted from MSBC 4343 Biblical Counseling Course at the College of Biblical Studies, Houston, Texas)

Biblical Framework Counseling: Its Universals

In his course of Biblical Counseling at the College of Biblical Studies Rich Thomson provides Seven universal Truths by which the Biblical Framework operates:

1. All people have an immaterial as well as a material aspect to their beings. It is in their immaterial beings (their souls and spirits – more commonly referred to in Scripture as their hearts) that they are qualitatively and uniquely different from the animals and in which they can relate to God (cf. Gen. 1:26). In their immaterial beings, all people are responsible to God for the thoughts, attitudes, words, and actions for which the Word of God states they are responsible (cf. Mk. 7:21-23).

    Because the biblical counselor understands these truths, he differentiates in his mind between the things for which the counselee is responsible to God and the things for which he is not responsible (cf. Job 1 & 2).

2. All people experience in their relationships and circumstances negative things which happen to them – for which they are not responsible to God (cf. Job 1& 2).

    The biblical counselor's responses to the negative things which have happened to the counselee should be to "weep with those who weep" (Rom. 12:15) and to "bear one another's burdens" (Gal. 6:2). Of course, positive things also happen to people, and in these the biblical counselor should "rejoice with those who rejoice" (Rom. 12:15). Rarely, however, do people seek counsel because things are going well.

3. All people experience non-responsible reactions to the positive and negative things which happen to them. That is, they experience physiological pain (and pleasure), immaterial grief or sorrow (and joy), and the bodily feelings which accompany them. These reactions are not wrong, and human beings are not responsible to God for them (cf. Eph. 4:30, I Pet. 2:23).

    Here the biblical counselor's response should be the same as that above – empathy.

4. When positive or negative things affect them, all people entertain either unloving or loving attitudes in their hearts in response to them and in response to the pain (or pleasure) and/or grief (or joy) which they experience as a result. Human beings are responsible to God for these reactions (cf. I Cor. 13:4-7).

    The biblical counselor's responsibility here is to praise the counselee's loving responses and – gently, at the appropriate time – to address the counselee's unloving responses as being sin before God (cf. I Thess. 5:14).

5. All people have a conscience which accuses them of their wrong responses and choices in life and exonerates them of their right responses and choices (cf. Rom. 2:15). As a result of the work of their consciences, then, they normally experience these instinctive and instantaneous immaterial effects in their hearts: a consciousness of guilt and a sense of guilt, or a consciousness of not being guilty and a sense of peace; a consciousness of God's judgment and a fear of that judgment, or a consciousness of approval and a sense of confidence; a fleeing from that sense of judgment and from that sense of guilt, or a drawing near to God (cf. Gen. 3:10-11, Prov. 28:1, I Jn. 4:18, Rom. 2:14-15).[*]

The biblical counselor's responsibility here is especially to recognize expressions of the negative effects in the counselee's life and to help him to understand and to deal with their root cause (cf. Prov. 20:5).

6. When people experience in their hearts a sense of guilt, a sense of judgment (usually experienced as apparently uncaused or disproportional fear – Prov. 28:1), or a fleeing from that sense of judgment (usually experienced as apparently uncaused or disproportional fleeing – Prov. 28:1), the only sufficient solution for the removal of these negative effects and their replacement with positive effects is a right relationship with the one true God made known through the Lord Jesus Christ (cf. Heb. 9:14, I Jn. 3:21).

The biblical counselor's responsibility here is to help the counselee understand his need for the forgiveness and righteousness provided by the Lord Jesus Christ (if he is an unbeliever) or his need for confession of his sin (if he is a believer) and the filling of God's Spirit, which happens concurrently with them, and which produces God's *agapē* love in his heart (cf. II Cor. 5:21, I Jn. 1:9, Eph. 5:18, Gal. 5:22-23).

7. There are four basic ways in which all people relate to each other.[**] At any given moment in any given relationship, they are either open and loving, open and unloving, closed and loving, or closed and unloving. (The unbeliever's love – reflected from God's good gifts in his life (cf. Jas. 1:17) – is but a faint representation of the love which the Holy Spirit produces in the believer's life.) (Cf. Prov. 27:5-6.)

The biblical counselor's responsibility here is to help the counselee see the importance of openly expressing God's love back to God and to his fellow man – at the proper time and place – and to guide the counselee in practical ways of openly expressing that love.

(Information adapted from MSBC 4343 Biblical Counseling Course at the College of Biblical Studies, Houston, Texas)

BIBLICAL COUNSELING FRAMEWORK

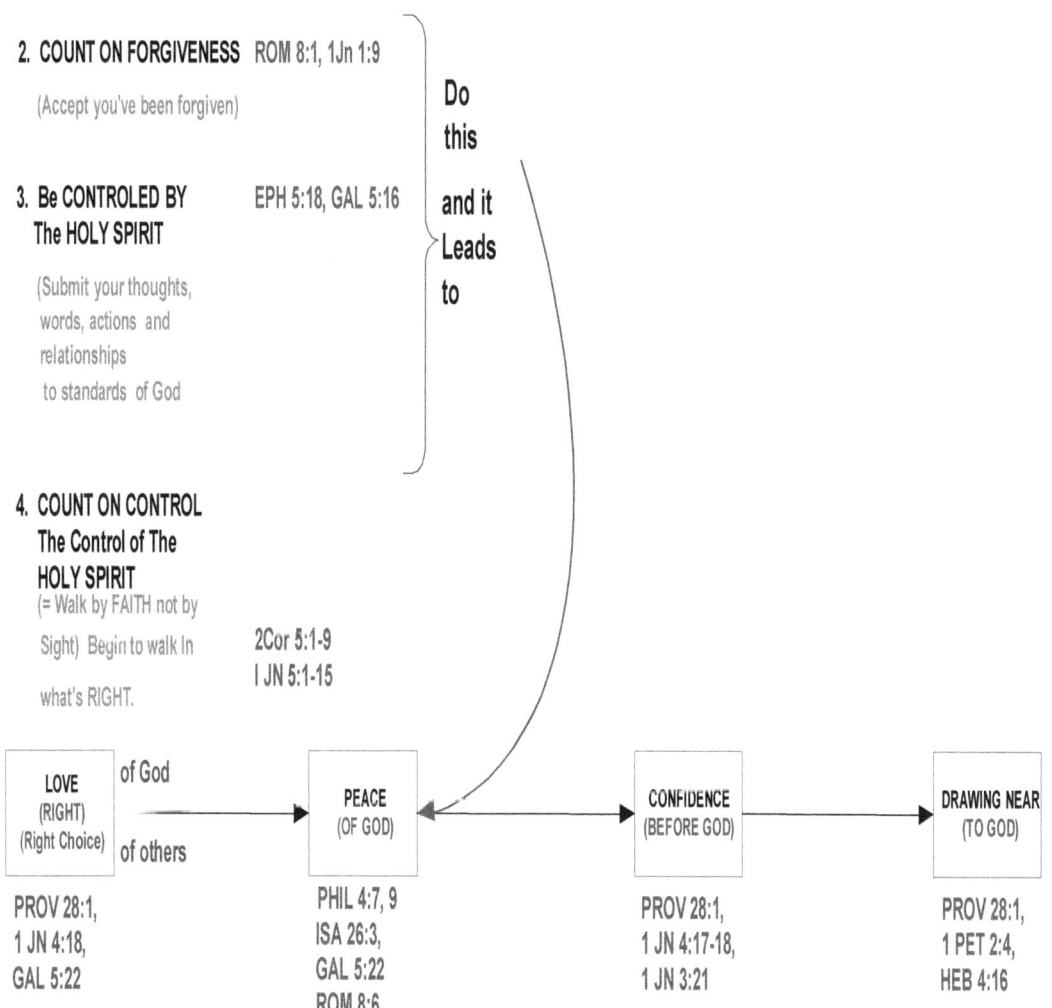

(Concept by Rich Thomson/ this picture of the Framework put together by Greg White)

Expressions

Key Point: Below is a list of ways in which a lack of love, guilt, uncaused fear, and uncaused fleeing tend to be expressed or demonstrated in everyday life situations. As we continue in our studies we will begin to use this terminology to explain how a lack of love, guilt, uncaused fear, and uncaused fleeing is being demonstrated in a person's life or in some case we will study. For instance we may say something such as:
 a. That is an expression(demonstration) of uncaused fleeing
 b. That is an expression(demonstration) of uncaused fear
 c. That is an expression (demonstration) of a sense of guilt
 d. That is an expression(demonstration) of a lack of love for God or others

This means that one of the elements of the framework is being expressed or demonstrated.

1. Lack of Love Expressions (Ways in which a lack of love may be expressed or demonstrated in everyday situations):

Impatience, irritability, annoyance, anger, rage, cruelty, unkindness, jealousy, envy, enmity, hostility, hatred, bragging, pride, conceit, immorality, impurity, indecency, criminality, thoughtlessness, greed, selfishness, stubbornness, obstinacy, self-centeredness, grumbling, thanklessness, discontentment, resentment, grudge-bearing, unforgiveness, bitterness, maliciousness, suspicion, pessimism, hopelessness

2. Guilt Expressions (Ways in which a sense of guilt may be expressed or demonstrated in everyday situations):

Feeling guilty, sense of condemnation, anticipation of punishment, bothered conscience, accusing thoughts, down on self, low self respect, sense of worthlessness, self condemnation, and excessive doubt about doing something

3. Uncaused Fear Expressions (Ways in which uncaused fear may be expressed in everyday situations):

Anxiety, uneasiness, apprehension, dread, tension, restlessness, excessive worry, anticipation of misfortune, danger or doom, irritability, over dependence, timidity, shyness, panic, terror, over concern, hyper-happiness, imagination of illness, agitation, over-activity, easy distraction, persecution complex.

When uncaused fear continues it may begin to affect the body. As a result one may begin to experience some physiological effects on the body because one is not dealing with their sin (Psalm 32:1-5). Some things which may be the physiological effects of uncaused fear are:

Hyper-alert, fidgety, talking to much, falling asleep, impaired concentration, poor memory, excessive perspiration, muscle tension, headaches, sighing respirations, hyperventilation, abdominal pain, nausea, diarrhea, butterflies, high blood pressure, rapid heartbeat, fainting episodes, frequent urination, impotence, frigidity, ulcers, nervous stomach, depletion of brain chemicals, hormone irregularities, weakened immune system.

4. Uncaused Fleeing Expressions (Ways in which uncaused fleeing may be expressed in everyday situations):

Withdrawal, isolation, escape, inner hiding, denial, defensiveness, excessive self protection, abandonment or denial of self evident truth, escape from reality, withdrawal of intimacy, embracing of fantasy as reality, pursuit of imaginary states, desperation to flood one's mind with stimuli, desperation to flood one's body with stimuli, anesthetizing one's brain, unwillingness to be open, living in a fantasy world, unwillingness to reason, delusions, blaming, self-justification, changing the subject, trying to get rid of another person

(Expressions derived from Minrith, Meier, and Rich Thomson)

Expressions of Love Homework Assignments

(Insight Adapted from <u>The Heart of Man and The Mental Disorders</u> by Rich Thomson)

1. Though man's heart is always transparent to God who knows all things, man should choose to express to God openly the love which draws him near to God in his heart. In other words, man should have an open loving relationship with God,

    A. Embracing who God is according to His Character/Attributes (Hebrews 11:6)
    B. Thinking on good things/Meditating on God's Word (Philippians 4:8)
    C. Accepting of what God has allowed in your life (Romans 8:28, 1Peter 5:6)
    D. Entrusting Oneself to God in doing/standing in what is right according to God's will in thoughts, words, behavior or lifestyle (1Peter 4:19, 1Corinthians 16:13-14)
    E. Thanksgiving for/in all things (Ephesians 5:20, 1 Thessalonians 5:18)
    F. Worship in Spirit and Truth (John 4:23-24, Hebrews 10:24-25)
    G. Praising God Constantly (Hebrews 13:15, Psalm 103:1, 150:106)
    H. Giving to God's Work (2 Corinthians 8:3-4, 8; 9:7)

2. An open loving relationship can be expressed to others in many ways at the right time, in the right way, in the right circumstance. (Proverbs 27:14; 25:11; 15:23; 15:1, Colossians 4:6)

    A. Sincere apologies (Matthew 5:23-24, Romans 12:18)
    B. Praising others (Proverbs 27:2, 31:28-29, 1 Corinthians 11:2)
    C. Listening and talking to them (James 1:19, Proverbs 18:2,13)
    D. Sharing where you hurt (2 Corinthians 6:11-13, 7:2-3)
    E. Spending time with one another (2 Corinthians 12:15, 1 Thessalonians 2:8,Ephesians 6:4, Titus 2:4-5)
    F. Gentle correction (Proverbs 27:6a, 1 Thessalonians 5:14)
    G. Self Sacrifice (1 Corinthians 13:5, Philippians 2:3-4)
    H. Submission to God ordained authority (Ephesians 5:22-6:9, Romans 13:1-7,Hebrews 13:17)
    I. Saying I love you (John 13:34)
    J. Giving encouragement (1 Thessalonians 5:11, 14, Proverbs 12:25)
    K. Showing appreciation (Philippians 4:14)
    L. Helping each other (Acts 20:35, 1 Thessalonians 5:14)
    M. Comforting each other (Romans 12:15, 2 Corinthians 1:3-4)
    N. Bearing one another's burden (Galatians 6:2)
    O. Warm smile or appropriate touch (Proverbs 15:30, Mark 10:13-14)
    P. Phoning or writing expressions of love (3 John 1:13-14)
    Q. Asking for help (Philippians 4:17)
    R. Expressing forgiveness when someone has apologized (2 Corinthians 2:7, Ephesians 4:32)
    S. Discipline of one's children (Ephesians 6:4, Proverbs 13:24)

T. Using your spiritual gifts to serve others (1 Peter 4:10-11)
U. Evangelism and Discipleship (Matthew 28:18-20, Ephesians 4:11-16)

3. Man should choose to express openly the love which God produces in his heart for his fellow man. In other words man should have open loving relationships with his fellow man. There are four kinds of human relationships: (Proverbs 27:5-6)

   a. Sometimes our relationships can be **open and unloving**. (v5)
      1. Rebuking others without respect.
      2. Exposing sin with rudeness.
      3. Exposing character flaws with harshness.
      4. Speaking truth with no love.

   b. Sometimes our relationships can be **closed and loving**. (v5)
      1. Appreciative but not expressing it.
      2. Concerned but not showing it.
      3. Having praise in heart but not expressing it.
      4. Desiring the highest good of others but not expressing it.

   c. Sometimes our relationships can be **open and loving**. (v6)
      1. Rebuking in love
      2. Spending quality time.
      3. Speaking the truth in love/giving encouragement.
      4. Meeting needs and bearing burdens.

   d. Sometimes our relationships can be **closed and unloving**. (v6)
      1. Talking behind someone's back instead of to them
      2. Insincere favors or gifts.
      3. Flattery
      4. Uncooperative

   e. How do we develop an **open and loving relationship**?
      1. Confess and repent of all unloving thoughts, words, and actions. (Proverbs 28:13-14)
      2. Begin speaking open expressions of love by faith. (Ephesians 4:15, 25, 29)
      3. Begin showing open expressions of love by faith.(1 Corinthians 13:4-8, Romans 12:9-21, 1 Peter 3:1-12, 1 Peter 4:7-11)
      4. Trust in God's power not your feelings or abilities.(Philippians 1:6, 2:12-16, 4:13, 2 Peter 1:2-3)

Ways We Can Embrace God

Characteristics of God to embrace	The Perspective We Should have as a result of embracing this Characteristic?	The Practice we should develop as result of embracing this Characteristic?	The Patterns of relating we should walk in as a result of embracing this Characteristic
Supreme – He is first and foremost before all things; all created things were designed to reflect the greatness of God; His glory is our goal. (Colossians 1:15-19)	I exist for His glory (Romans 11:36}	Live for the audience of God alone, Put God first (1Corinthains 10:31)	Consider God's Glory not your personal gain when relating to others (Philippians 2:1-4)
Sovereign - God controls all things; nothing happens unless God allows it or ordains it; He upholds all things by His power (Ecclesiastes 7:13-14)	My life is in the hands of God and He has it under control (Ecclesiastes 9:1)	Trust God with all your heart by focusing on what you are called to do and stop trying to play God with your circumstances (Proverbs 3: 5-8)	Stop trying to control what others think, say, and do in relation to you or with anything and accept your role under God with them (Matthew 22:34-40)
Sufficient – God is enough and He is doing enough in relation to my life (Psalm 145:17-21)	God is enough and He is doing enough for me (Psalm 73:25-28)	Enjoy what God provides without complaining about what you do not have (Philippians 4:10-14)	Give to others knowing God will supply your needs (Luke 6:30-36)
Holy – unique and set apart from sin while dedicated to His glory (Isaiah 6:1-4)	I must be in the world but be set apart for Christ (1Peter 1:13-16)	Present your body as a living and holy sacrifice to God (Romans 12:1)	Treat others as precious and valuable to God (1Thessalonians 4:1-8)
Loving – seeks the highest good of others; gives himself for the good of others; gives himself to be a blessing to others (Romans 5:8-11)	God is always looking out for me no matter what happens (Hebrews 13:5-6)	Live to be blessing to God (1Corinthians 10:31)	Bear burdens and meet needs of others (Galatians 6:1-2, Titus 3:14)
Wise – He knows and works the best course of action to bring about His greatest glory and our greatest good (Job 9:4-12)	God knows how to bring about the best results for my life (Romans 8:28-39)	Listen to God and follow Him accordingly (Ecclesiastes 5:1-2)	Listen to others with the intent to learn what to do or what not to do accordingly (Proverbs 18:15)
Gracious – showing favor, being a benefit and being generous to people who deserve punishment without them having to earn it or work for it (Ephesians 2:8-10)	I will receive blessings that I don't deserve because of my relationship with God (Psalm 103:1-8)	Give thanks to God and enjoy what He provides (1Thessaloninas 5:18)	Be kind and beneficial to people who don't deserve it (Luke 6:30-36)
Merciful – not giving people the punishment they deserve (2Samuel 24:14-25)	God is always cutting me slack (Psalm 103:9-10)	Repent of all known sin accordingly to God (2Corinthians 7:10-11)	Cut people some slack without dismissing their sin (Romans 12:17-18)
Forgiving – canceled the debt owed by sin; will not hold sin against us (Psalm 103:1-14)	God will always forgive if I ask for it (1John 1:9)	Confess sins to God accordingly (Psalm 32:1-5)	Forgive others as you have been forgiven by God (Matthew 18:21-35)
Faithful – God will always be true to His Word; He will always do whatever He says or promises (Numbers 23:19)	The Lord will never leave me nor forsake me He will always be there (Hebrews 13:5-6)	Serve God faithfully while continuing to wait on His return (1Corinthains 15:58)	Be faithful to others according to the level of the relationship (Proverbs 27:6)

Eight "C"s of Biblical Counseling

1. **_Connect_** with the counselee in the first part of the counseling session.
   a. Ask your counselee questions that will help you to get to know them better
   b. Identify areas of common interest and share those with the counselee
   c. Share things about yourself that you think will lead your counselee to be comfortable with you (Proverbs 16:24))

2. **_Console_** the Counselee during the counseling session.
   a. Give words of hope and encouragement to assure the counselee that God has solutions to their problem
   b. Provide comfort as the counselee shares their problems and concerns
   c. Be compassionate and patient as your counselee shares their heart with you

3. **_Collect_** data from the Counselee in regards to their problems and concerns.
   a. Find out what is happening or has happened to the person.
   b. Find out how they are responding in thought, words, behavior, lifestyle, relational patterns to what is happening or has happened.
   c. Identify time frame of responses to people, places, events in accordance to what is happening or has happened
   d. Find out what they want that they cannot control getting and what they are getting they do not want.
   e. Identify areas of anger, worry, or fear
   f. Find out what the person's perceptions, preferences, pains, passions are in connection to what is happening or has happened
   g. Find out how they have dealt with or are dealing with sin towards God and others.
   h. Look for any and all unloving attitudes, words, and actions

4. **_Categorize_** data from the Counselee into Biblical terms and perspectives as you are thinking through Biblical solutions.
   a. Where there is a biblical term or interpretation for the data use it in place of psychological terms so that those issues may be dealt with accordingly.
   b. Identify and interpret data that is an expression of apparently uncaused fleeing as such when you are collecting the data.
   c. Identify and interpret data that is an expression of apparently uncaused fear as such when you are collecting the data.
   d. Identify and interpret data that is an expression of a sense of guilt as such when you are collecting the data.
   e. Identify and interpret first level and second level sins, root sins and fruit sins as such when you are collecting the data
   f. Identify and interpret what a person can and cannot control in their situation past, present, future as you are collecting the data
   g. Identify and interpret their conduct, character, and conversation according to Biblical perspectives

5. **Communicate** to Counselee what the Bible defines as the source and the symptoms of the problems in Biblical terms and *clarify* what the Biblical solutions are to those problems.
   a. Explain the concept of a lack of love for God and others and the solution of love.
   b. Explain the concept of two-level sins and the solution to this.
   c. Explain the concept of idolatrous-lust and the solutions to this.
   d. Explain the concept of progressive sanctification.
   e. Explain the concept of confession, repentance, and replacement.
   f. Explain the material and immaterial issues of man.
   g. Explain the concept of guilt and the standards of the conscience.
   h. Explain the four kinds of human relationships.
   i. Explain the fear of man, anger, worry, anxiety and the solutions.
   j. Explain the concept of pride and the solutions.
   k. Explain the concept of embracing God according to who He is.
   l. Explain the concept of what a man can and cannot control and how to work through that in a practical manner.
   m. Explain the control of the Holy Spirit

6. **Challenge** the Counselee to a commitment to confess, repent, and replace sin with love for God and others.
   a. Ask the counselee if they are willing to do the hard work of confessing, repenting, replacing sin with love for God and others.
   b. Explain to the counselee the importance of being a doer of the Word and not just a hearer of the Word.
   c. Explain what kind of commitment it will take to make the appropriate changes to resolve the problem and become Godly in the situation.

7. **Construct** homework for the counselee to apply to their lives that will lead them into confession, repentance, and replacement of sin with love for God and others

   a. *Hope Homework* – projects, activities and reading assignments given to help people gain a true hope in Christ in accordance to the problems they are facing

   b. *Doctrinal Homework* – projects, activities, and reading assignments given to help people gain a solid theological understanding of their problems so that they can deal with them properly

   c. *Awareness Homework* – projects, activities, and reading assignments given to help people become aware of their own sinfulness in the problem so that they can stop deceiving themselves about the problem they are facing and own up to it accordingly

d. ***Embracing God Homework*** – projects, activities, and reading assignments given to help people to connect with God according to a particular characteristic of God that relates to their problem or sin

e. ***Action Oriented Homework*** – projects and activities that lead people to put off particular sinful thoughts, desires, conversations, behavior, and lifestyle and to put on particular godly thoughts, desires, conversations, behavior, and lifestyle that according to the situation or problem

f. ***Relational Orientated Homework*** – projects and activities that lead people to put off unloving relational patterns and move them to relate in open and loving relational patterns towards others within the situation or problem and abroad

(Portions of this information was adapted from *Instruments in a Redeemer's Hand* by Paul Tripp)

8. ***Conjoin*** the counselee to the Body of Christ according to where they need it.

    a. *Membership* – the counselee would be lead to join a local church that they may experience love and enjoy the blessings of God-honoring relationships.

    b. *Maturity* – the counselee would be lead to get involved in discipleship courses in a local Church that would lead them into loving God, loving others on a consistent basis and living a life that reflects the character of Christ.

    c. *Magnification* – the counselee would be led to come to appreciate, value and adore the character of God through heart-felt genuine worship of Him in a local Church.

    d. *Ministry* – the counselee would be led to join a ministry where they can develop in bearing burdens and meeting needs according to the various relationships they will develop through the local Church

    e. *Missions* – the counselee would be led into supporting a local Church in sharing and defending the Christian faith

Bibliography

Adams, Jay. How to Help People Change, Grand Rapids, Zondervan, 1986

Adams, Jay Solving Marriage Problems, Grand Rapids, Zondervan, 1983

Thomson, Rich. The Heart of Man and The Mental Disorders, Houston: Biblical Counseling Ministries, Inc., 2004

Tripp, Paul David. Instruments in the Redeemer's Hands: People in Need of Change Helping People in Need of Change, Phillipsburg, NJ: P&R, 2002.

MSBC 4343 Biblical Counseling Course at the College of Biblical Studies, Houston, Texas)

www.ingramcontent.com/pod-product-compliance
Lightning Source LLC
Chambersburg PA
CBHW081233170426
43198CB00017B/2746